Jean-Marie Pinçon

Nicolas Feuillatte

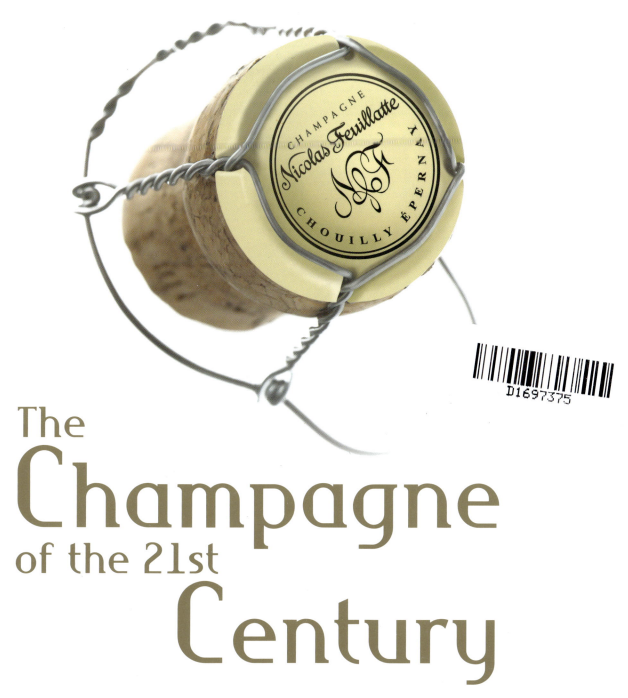

The Champagne of the 21st Century

THALIA
EDITION

Jean-Marie Pinçon

Nicolas Feuillatte

The Champagne of the 21st Century

THALIA
EDITION

Cover Illustration: *The Nicolas Feuillatte Cork,* 2010. © Baptiste Heller.

Editorial Direction: Aleksandra Sokolov

Editing and Typesetting: Jean-Marie Pinçon and Aurore Markowski

Proofreading: Pascale Braud

Translator: Valentina Relton

www.expressit.org

Concept and Design:
Studio Ma Graphiste, Paris
Aurore Markowski
www.magraphiste.fr

Graphic Designers: Graphium, Paris
www.graphium.fr

Isbn: 978-2-35278-089-2

SUMMARY

- Preface 7
- Prologue 8

PART ONE:
A UNIQUE STORY 10

- An arduous path towards cooperation . 12
- The Foundation 26
- The building work 38
- A major challenge 52
- The turning point 64
- The ramifications continue 76

PART TWO:
MODERN TIMES 86

- The Conquest of a Global Market .. 88
- 2000-2010, a decade of paradoxes ... 104
- An Eye to the Future? 122

PART THREE:
GREATER GOALS 132

- An avant-garde facility 135
- The linchpin: the cellar master 146
- Audacity and communication 168

- References 186
- Acknowledgements 187
- Nota Bene 187
- Iconographical index 188

Nicolas Feuillatte. The champagne bearing his name is a worldwide brand and the top seller in France.

PAGE 6 | Nicolas Feuillatte, the champagne of the 21st Century

Preface

Sylvain Delaunois, President of the Centre Vinicole - Champagne Nicolas Feuillatte once said that "One must steep oneself in one's past to be a part of the future![1]"

This book presents me with the opportunity to unveil the history of CV – CNF spanning from its origins to the present day. It is an account of the formidable and legendary champagne to which I have given my name. I am proud of the path we have taken, and of my desire to share my beloved nectar with friends.

If in less than forty years production levels have risen from several million to tens of millions of Nicolas Feuillatte champagne enjoyed all over the world, it is because of the generosity of spirit of the people I have had the pleasure to work with, ardent defenders of their chosen path, eager to produce a champagne of superb quality and devoted to their mission to maximise a sustainable revenue potential for each and every member of the Centre Vinicole, thus creating an outlet for their investment. This noble feat has been accomplished.

With humility they have also paved the way to find a balance between themselves and the buyers, who traditionally are the key players in champagne.

I would like to take this opportunity to thank everyone who has played a part in charting the history of Nicolas Feuillatte. The company's history and mine are one and the same. It is my express wish that I look forward to seeing future generations steeping themselves in the past so that they may, in turn, play a role in our future.

Nicolas Feuillatte

[1]. Sylvain Delaunois was at the time the President of the Fédération des coopératives vinicoles of the Champagne. The statement was published in the editorial of a paper published marking the 60th anniversary of the FCVC in 1999.

"A winery nestling on twelve hectares of land ... an armoury of stainless steel, thermo-regulated vats with a 304,000 hectolitre capacity ... 20,000 bottles filled per hour ... 100,000,000 bottles laid down in our cellars at any given point in time ... 500,000 bottles riddled by gyropalettes a week ... 9,000 bottles disgorged per hour ... 9,000 bottles labelled per hour ... then mechanically boxed by three machines ..."

Prologue

These figures may appear to border on excess, and may come as a surprise to the at times incredulous visitor to our Centre Vinicole - Champagne Nicolas Feuillatte. Yet his disbelief is perfectly understandable when he discovers that this formidable enterprise has not yet celebrated its fortieth birthday.

"You are about to witness the operation of an exceptional organisation whose philosophy aims towards utmost transparency …" The tour guide goes straight to the point. With the minimum of fuss she prepares the ground for a "fragrantly candid visit, the like of which is not generally available to most visitors".

The tour of the cellars is what one would expect of a great, classic champagne house. The visitor descends to its chalk pits (crayères), underground chambers dating from the pre-Middle Ages. Nicolas Feuillatte broke with strongly embedded touristic and commercial traditions by setting up a cooperative in Chouilly that is both educative and a joy to see in action. The majority of the cellars here are on ground level[2], which is most unusual in the Champagne region, though common in many other wine regions. Because of the advancement of technology we can today recreate an ideal self-contained environment by regulating temperatures, humidity levels and shade found naturally in the centuries' old chalk pits. The catacombs and sepulchral atmosphere of the Chouilly of old did not sit well with the efficiency of modern technology. The traditional spirit, what the French call l'esprit, will always be part of the cooperative as long as it adds quality and value to the product. The crystalline clinks of the bottles combined with the metallic whirrings of the conveyor belt briefly interrupt the commentary. The aim of this guided tour giving me unprecedented access to the Chouilly cellars and consisting of a succession of beautifully narrated stop-off points, is to explain clearly and simply the processes that go into making Nicolas Feuillatte champagne. My foray into the world of oenology is elucidated by my guide who cleverly illustrates her tour with notice boards providing a concisely worded potted history, photographic images and simple graphics to make it all as clear as possible. Therein lie two to the secrets of the success of this exceptional wine, the third being a succession of life-sized paintings depicting the various compartments

---

2. In order to comply with energy saving policies, the newest cellars installed in 2009 are underground. See chapter "An avant-garde facility".

of this huge complex, such as the majestic cuverie housing gigantic steel tanks, the astounding riddling hall equipped with pirouetting gyropalettes, the metronomic dancing of the disgorging machine, the procession of bottles swallowed up by see-through cubicles where the labelling takes place … these are just some of the remarkable processes that go into making champagne.

This book also provides a meticulous summary of the history of the Centre Vinicole, a shining tribute to the work of the 4,500 members of the CV-CNF, (one in three winegrowers in the region belongs to the cooperative), a glowing assessment of the quality of the supplies (the finest crus of Montagne de Reims, Côte des Blancs, Vallée de la Marne and Côte des Bars) and a limpid account of the combined energies of each cooperative member (the Centre Vinicole is made up of 83 individual cooperatives locking the union together). And lastly, a clear reminder of the company's statistics enabling us to understand Nicolas Feuillatte's position as a global market leader. All this makes for an impressive calling card for one of the five top champagne houses in the world.

My guide is unequivocal: ("This cuvée will fill 133,000 bottles …") she proudly states, ("You are standing in front of the fastest piece of machinery in the entire Champagne region …"), an affirmation dispelling fears felt by many ("We've maintained the industry quality standard since 1996 …", "A fully operational water treatment plant capable of supplying a town with 27,000 inhabitants …"), with a touch of humour ("Here we are, as it were, in the playroom of Jean-Pierre Vincent, our Cellar Master, this is after all where he creates his different blends …").

My guide effortlessly tells me everything I need to know during my visit[3], and the time flies by, travelators and elevators facilitating our tour of the premises. I complete the last leg of the tour, inspecting the state of the art equipment and row upon row of champagne bottles. This is a thoroughly modern set up geared towards upholding the standards set Nicolas Feuillatte, a unique patrimony gathered together in storerooms boasting row upon row of millions of bottles that testify to the vitality of the Centre Vinicole. As we stop and talk at perhaps another ten locations my understanding of the champagne industry as a thoroughly modern concern evolving with the times consolidates. The potential today's technology has to offer the industry is yet to be realised. Following our "theoretical" appetizer, much like the cherry on the cake, is the practical business of various tasting options, depending on the tour the visitor takes. This final stage in the tour provides the ultimate proof that champagne need not be enjoyed on special occasions, the sipping of this exceptional wine is something to be cherished in itself. This tour has without question taken me beyond the traditional champagne circuit; it has led to a more truthful and honest experience, which has opened my eyes to today's champagne industry. In order to gain a deeper understanding of the Centre and its meteoric growth, my voyage of discovery can only be completed by going back in time and recounting the thirty eight year history of Nicolas Feuillatte Champagne.

3. The visit lasts approximately one and a half hours

Up until the second half of the twentieth century the winegrower from the Champagne wine growing region of France was put simply a grape grower whose business was largely dependent upon the buyer, who was in effect the sole autocrat of the champagne market. At the turn of the 1900's a handful of men involved in setting up the fledgling unionist movement were convinced that the cooperative movement would lead to greater self sufficiency, enabling the winegrowers to "make a living from their products". In other words, it offered a guarantee that his wines would be sold and, if possible, at the right price.

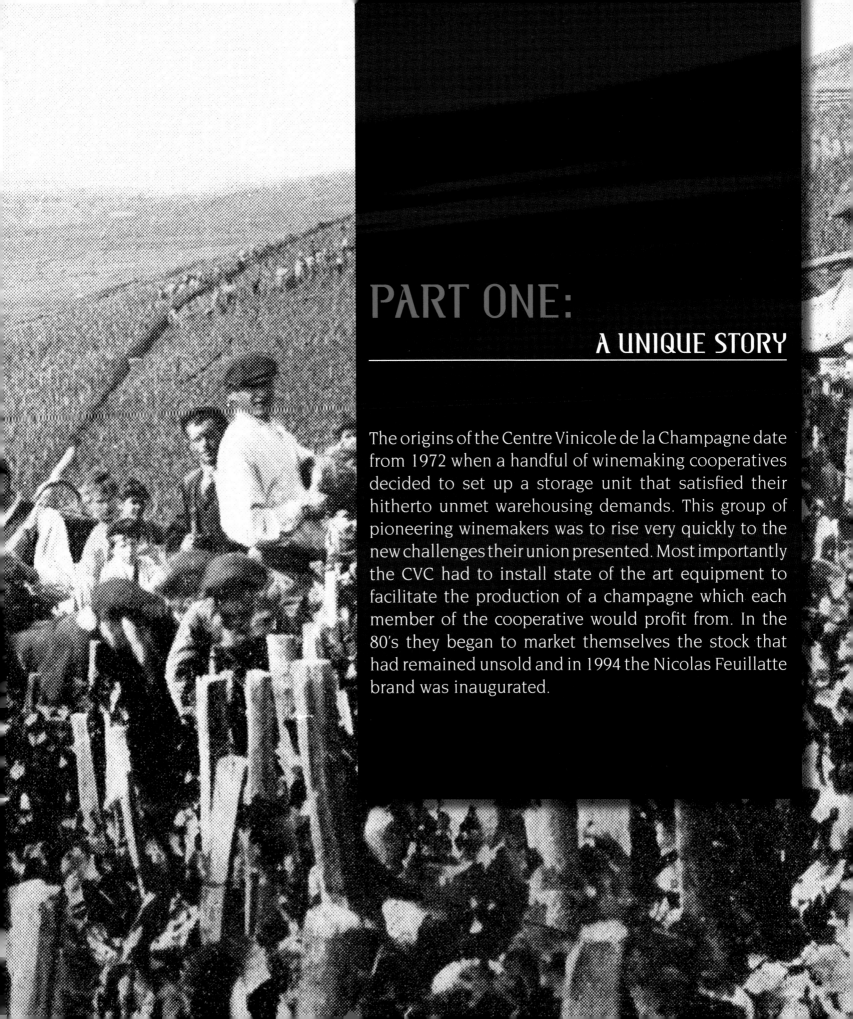

PART ONE:
A UNIQUE STORY

The origins of the Centre Vinicole de la Champagne date from 1972 when a handful of winemaking cooperatives decided to set up a storage unit that satisfied their hitherto unmet warehousing demands. This group of pioneering winemakers was to rise very quickly to the new challenges their union presented. Most importantly the CVC had to install state of the art equipment to facilitate the production of a champagne which each member of the cooperative would profit from. In the 80's they began to market themselves the stock that had remained unsold and in 1994 the Nicolas Feuillatte brand was inaugurated.

Pictured across the front cover of the weekly magazine *Paris illustré* of 5th November 1887 was an image of a harvest in full swing in Champagne. The artist Maybach depicted a winegrower and his partner dressed in the costumes of the time working around the vine stocks laden with grapes. The reality of the situation was at the time far less rosy than the image this idyllic depiction portrayed.

At the turn of the 1990's the winegrowers tried to protect their vines against disease and pests, yet the phylloxera epidemic was too great and not a single vine stock was saved. The winegrowers in the Champagne wine region were ravaged by this indestructible aphid.

20. Ay et sa côte

The origins of The Centre Vinicole - Champagne Nicolas Feuillatte are steeped in the tradition of wine producing cooperatives and today it is one of the leading innovators in the industry. Run by a group of highly gifted and enterprising individuals, the cooperative has always been one step ahead of its time. These are just a few of the reasons behind its success.

An arduous path towards cooperation

The adventure began with the outstanding vintage of 1970, an extraordinary year[4]. The Champagne region simply did not have the equipment to press the grapes or the facilities for storing the must[5]. Yet this was not the first time that a lack of equipment had been a region-wide dilemma. The newly-formed Champagne winegrowers Union[6] (Le Syndicat des vignerons de la Champagne) had in 1921 conducted a survey exposing the weaknesses at regional level. The biggest issue they faced was the chronic lack of storage which resulted in the winegrowers being overly dependent on buyers over whom they were virtually powerless[7]. The formation of a cooperative was deemed by the union bosses to be the only viable way of dealing with the region's problems.

4. See "The Foundation" Chapter.
5. Must is pre-fermented grape juice.
6. The Syndicat général des vignerons de la Champagne (SGVC) followed on from the Fédération des vignerons in 1919 which had been set up in 1904.
7. In the Champagne industry, the buyers (or "négoce") are the historic houses trading in champagne and the "negociants manipulateurs" once they've vinified the grapes into champagne then sell the bottles.

Part one - A unique story | PAGE 13

The formation of cooperatives had been widely discussed in the early 1990's. Cooperatives had had associations with the champagne union since its inception. As early as 1912, Alphonse Perrin[8], Secretary of the SGVC, stated that "The future and prosperity of Champagne lie within a union and system of cooperatives". The following year, Gaston Poittevin[9] foresaw a cooperative system as one providing economical advantages. "By forming cooperatives we can apply the law of supply and demand." Lamenting the failed discussion on pricing issues held two years earlier with buyers he quoted Alphonse Perrin who hoped to "rally (my) fellow winegrowers and form with them a cooperative in order to combat if necessary the intransigence of those trading in Champagne wines." It was a few years earlier that another key player in the Champagne union, Émile Michel-Lecacheur[10], asserted that the formation of a cooperative was the only way to guarantee the future of the winegrower "a slave to the plot of land inherited from his fathers, who sacrificed everything in order to pass it on to his children[11]".

Clearly, according to the Union, the cooperative would make the winegrower self sufficient, allowing him to "make a living from his work". In short, he would be confident that he would be able to sell his product and, if possible, at the right price. At that time the producer was put simply a grape grower whose work depended entirely upon buyers, who were in effect the autocrats of the Champagne wine market. When it came to purchasing the grapes, they were the ones setting the price and could chose to buy just a small amount. As a consequence, negotiations were biased in favour of the purchaser. Several discussions were held between the Syndicat and the traders, but each time negotiations failed due to the lack of equality between the sovereign buyer and his dependent, the seller.

The Great War of 1914-1918 did to a certain extent reverse the situation. After the armistice, mentalities changed throughout society. The winemakers of Champagne now more than ever before steadfastly

In 1912, Alphonse Perrin, the secretary of the Syndicat général des vignerons de la Champagne (the SGVC), stated that "The future and prosperity of Champagne lie within a union and system of cooperatives".

believed that the secret to their future lay in "a healthy economy for the winegrowers", and in the wake of some rather feeble attempts to set up a cooperative in the pre-war era, they got the first cooperatives off the ground, the result of which were champagnes made collectively by Avenay, Champillon and Cumières[12]. The process was nevertheless fraught with difficulties.

Up until then, their primary concern was to have at their disposal sufficiently large stockrooms to store overstocks of unsold grapes which they then vinified.

8. Alphonse Perrin (1875 - 1928).
9. Gaston Poittevin (1880-1944), representative of the cooperative at la Marne from 1919 to 1936. He was president of the Syndicat des vignerons de la Champagne between 1938 and 1941. He died in a concentration camp.
10. Émile Joseph Michel-Lecacheur (1871-1921).
11. In *La Champagne viticole*, November 1911.
12. François Bonal in *Le Livre d'or du champagne*.

Selling directly to the consumer was not illegal and it is what they had been doing[13], individually and on a much smaller scale, since 1900. René Lamarre had attempted to set up a cooperative in Damery in 1891, but it was to fold only two years later in 1893[14]. The commercial aspects for growers working on a small scale were fraught with difficulties: the cost of materials and equipment were beyond their pockets and the geographical area in which they operated was tiny (incorporating perhaps one or two communes). This hindered producers no end; their supplies were limited which impacted upon the quality of grapes they could use and commercial channels simply did not exist outside the network of friends and family.

A large scale cooperative with an extensive membership would lead to far greater self sufficiency and reduce the obstacles faced by producers. Each member would see a greater yield from his investment, and loans would be much easier to obtain. Lastly, with a qualitatively attractive production mechanism in place, wine could be made with different crus as is widely practised by buyers. But only one cooperative operating on a region wide scale could fulfil these conditions: the COGEVI, the first Champagne cooperative set up in Dizy[15] in September 1921. Mobilized by their union representatives, the producers were eager to join. The trade publication La Champagne viticole also encouraged those outside the union network to buy

Émile Michel-Lecacheur (1), another key figure in the Champagne union movement asserted that the formation of a cooperative was the only way to guarantee the future of the winegrower. Gaston Poittevin (2), a winegrower and future representative of the cooperative at la Marne regarded the cooperative system as one providing economical advantages.

13. "manipuler" is the word used by the champagne industry to mean the process of making champagne, seeing through all the various processes that go into making the end product.
14. In the work *100 Ans d'unité syndicale*, 1904-2004, published to celebrate the 100th anniversary of the SGVC, Yves Chauvé wrote that René Lamarre (1870 - ?) had laid down the foundations for a union that was to be involved in both making and selling champagne. The Champagne historian François Bonal identified a "super-cooperative" in 1898, founded by the winegrower from Damery which could attract the membership of other Champagne winegrowers in the book *Le Livre d'or du champagne*.
15. Founded in Dizy, the Société coopérative producing and selling still wine and champagne made by the Champagne viticole was to become the Coopérative Générale des Vignerons. Today, the COGEVI's headquarters are in Aÿ.

wines made by its members, saying that by helping COGEVI they were helping themselves (the future of Champagne can only be safeguarded by widespread cooperation").

The role played by the cooperation in society as a whole, quite apart from its economic relevance, was at the forefront of the members' objectives. Not only did it guarantee employment to its farming members by giving them an alternative outlet, it also provided recruitment possibilities, as this small advert published by the press in 1923 states: "COGEVI is looking for brokers paid on commission to find outlets for its white wines and Crémant de Champagne[16]." Moreover, and well ahead of its time, it gave employment to the physically impaired: "Physically disabled producers […], please make enquiries at the Head Office of COGEVI." Other cooperatives were soon to follow suit, such as the L'indépendante de Festigny, set up by Marcel Berthelot[17] in 1927. Initially the cooperative dealt with grape pressing, but four years later, in 1931 it diversified and performed the whole vinification process when it became known as the Union des Viticulteurs de Festigny[18]. Innovators, the cooperative members, right from the start, built with their own hands vinification tanks made from … concrete, with mixed results. The Coopérative des Grands Crus founded in Reims in 1926 folded in 1978[19] in the aftermath of the first major petrol crisis. However the Société de Producteurs set up in Mailly in 1929 is very much a thriving concern today[20] run as a cooperative by winemakers. When in 1930 buyers were few and far between, the members of the cooperative decided it was time to produce their own champagne. But in order to do this they needed bottles and more crucially a cellar to transform and age the wine into champagne. They got their bottles with the help of the locals and the cellars they had to excavate their own underground chambers themselves. With remarkable determination they, armed with pickaxes and shovels, and after a demanding day's work out on the vineyard, excavated out their vaults, drilling their cellars and saving them from disbanding.

Maurice Doyard, secretary general of the SGVC re-iterated in 1937 that "the key to the future of Champagne rests in the cooperative's ability to produce a quality wine".

16. "Crémant" was formerly champagne with a less generous mousse, with a creamy soft feel to it. Today, crémant is a sparkling wine made in a similar way to champagne but with less pressure.
17. Marcel Eugène Berthelot (1886-1975) also founded on 3rd June 1939 the Fédération des coopératives vinicoles de la Champagne.
18. It had 75 members in 1937, who farmed 90% of the wine growing land in the district.
19. The Cooperative was primarily known for making champagne Castille.
20. Mailly Grand Cru has gone from strength to strength, with 83 cooperative members involved in its making spread over 70 hectares of vineyards. This dynamic cooperative is quite separate from the Centre Vinicole.

This early 19th century postcard shows grapes being harvested from vine stocks planted in their droves and in no particular order, as was customary in days gone by. It was only after the phylloxera epidemic that grapevines were replanted in straight lines, a system much favoured today.

2. VENDANGE EN CHAMPAGNE — La Cueillette du raisin

With common interest at heart

Cooperatives take hold in the Champagne region. Yet, because of the very nature of the agricultural world to which they belong, many producers defend their desire for independence, so much so that the vast majority steer clear of the budding move towards unionisation. At the outbreak of the Second World War there were only thirty cooperatives operating in Champagne. Their influence was limited. The traders' power remained intact despite the difficulties of the 1930's. When the money is there to buy grapes from winegrowers, the surplus of stocks and lack of storage space accounts for the buyers' reticence. The phenomenon is aggravated by the fact that 1934 and 1935 were exceptionally good years, both in terms of quality and yield, which meant that the champagne producers could only salvage a small percentage of their god sent nectar.

The future of champagne is in jeopardy, and everyone involved, winegrowers and buyers, stands up and takes notice. When Maurice Doyard[21] spoke at the Syndicat des vignerons 1937 general meeting he said "the key to the future of Champagne rests in the cooperative's ability to produce a quality wine", Robert-Jean de Vogüé[22] wrote shortly afterwards in Le Vigneron champenois: "We must establish a network of cooperatives controlled at regional level if we want to resolve the problems faced by the champagne industry under the guidance of a professional organisation."

21. Maurice Doyard (1889-1974), secretary general of the SGVC between 1925 and 1939.
22. Robert-Jean de Vogüé (1896 - 1976), president of the employers of Moët & Chandon, was right from the very start in the 1930's (together with Gaston Martin, president of the employees) an exemplary speaker on social issues. He was instrumental in setting up the contract that paved the way for collective standards shared by all the Champagne house.

In the 1930's, the determined winegrowing cooperative members armed themselves with pickaxes and shovels. The producers of Mailly in the Marne (today Mailly Grand Cru) excavated their cellars after a demanding day's work in the vineyard. The cooperative members at Festigny built their own tanks out of concrete.

The Second World War presented new causes for concern in the industry. But it is important to remember that the legal approval granted on 12th April 1941 and then enforced by decree the following 8th September led to the setting up of the Comité interprofessionnel du vin de Champagne (the CIVC), the body representing the interests of all professionals working in the field, namely the winegrowers, buyers and cooperatives, staff, brokers and those working in associated industries[23]. Robert-Jean de Vogüé in his elected role as President was responsible for negotiations with buyers and Maurice Doyard, his Co-President, represented the producers. In 1945, de Vogüé is arrested by the Gestapo and imprisoned. He was replaced by René Chayoux[24], and Albert Dagonnet[25] succeeded Maurice Doyard in 1944.

During Liberation the slate was wiped clean with regards to institutions, bodies and regulations set up during the Occupation, and so, the future of the CIVC was in jeopardy. Above and beyond the high esteem with which they regarded Robert de Vogüé which led to their widespread support of this now free man, many Champagne producers felt there was a need to regulate contractual relations between the parties, "so that effort may be fairly rewarded". Moreover, the CIVC,

23. The forerunner of the CIVC was set up in November 1940 by the Bureau national de la répartition des vins de Champagne (BRC) which in turn had been instituted by the Vichy government wanting to set up a strengthened body representing the professionals in the industry. It was headed up by two men representing the buyers (Robert-Jean de Vogüé and Marcel Bouché) and two men representing the winegrowers (Maurice Berthelot and Maurice Doyard).
24. René Chayoux (1892 – 1969), co-president of the CIVC from 1944 to 1953.
25. Albert Dagonnet (1884 – 1970).

founded on sound principles, provided invaluable perspectives that resulted in positive measures then taken up by key players. One in particular, Henri Macquart[26], a partisan for change, made some radical policy changes. Following on from an analysis of the common interest of the winegrowers and buyers who, amongst other things, fiercely guarded the appellation contrôlée system, encouraged research in winemaking and the structure of inter-professional relations, Henri Macquart discussed his decision with his colleagues in the Syndicat, asking them to carry on with the CIVC. But because the current climate of the time was one of marked hostility, trying to convince the most sceptic was no easy task. It was at this point in time that the honest producer from Pourcy made his mark in the history of champagne. Other visionary courses of action that were to radically modify the landscape of the industry were soon to follow. Elected President of the Syndicat des vignerons the following year, Henri Macquart went on to playing a major role in the cooperative movement and in improving inter-professional relations. With Jean Nollevalle[27] as the permanent secretary of the SGVC, he developed a phenomenal network of contacts in the 1950's. His legitimacy as a producer (his family estate boasted a 150 year heritage), qualifications (he was a agricultural engineer), natural self-confidence and common sense, his first hand experience with cooperatives and unbiased view of the world of champagne all contributed towards conveying his unimpeachable authority when in negotiations with unions and the authorities. The CIVC, of which he is co-president for fourteen years, working mainly alongside René Chayoux and subsequently with Christian Heidsieck[28], finds in him an able and well respected negotiator. Besides, Louis Budin[29] and Robert-Jean de Vogüé, both later appointed as president of the Association viticole champenoise[30], and equally passionate about the future of champagne were also highly eloquent speakers.

The president of Moët & Chandon, Robert-Jean de Vogüé wrote himself in *Le Vigneron champenois* that "We must establish a network of cooperatives controlled at regional level ..."

---

26. Henri Macquart (1914 – 2005).
27. Jean Nollevalle (1917 – 2005). Permanent Secretary of the Syndicat général des vignerons for thirty years. He was mainly responsible for commissioning research and conceiving ideas. His influence is widely felt today.
28. Christian Heidsieck (1897 – 1982).
29. Louis Budin (1884 – 1972).
30. The Association viticole champenoise (AVC) was set up in 1989 by the buyers in a bid to combat the grape phylloxera pest. Its members today include winegrowers, cooperatives and champagne houses. Its mission is to encourage and develop innovation with utmost respect for quality and to disseminate technical information to everyone operating in the sector, particularly through the magazine *Le Vigneron champenois*.

Mastering Champagne making

The cooperative movement is a priority for Henri Macquart. In the aftermath of the WWII one in two producers is a member of a cooperative. In 1950 the Fédération des coopératives viticoles de Champagne has 50 members; by 1960, just 10 years later, the number rose to 110, equating to approximately 40% of the land cultivated by producers. In 1955, with sales hitting the 4 million mark, champagne making is a big deal for winegrowers but a major concern for champagne houses. Lucid, the Union Leader, whilst clearly satisfied with the healthy state of the market is nevertheless concerned. If, as clearly stated by Jean Nollevalle in December "The winegrower is even more in control of the situation […], does the work of a wine made in a few barrels and not in a cellar but in a cluttered storeroom result in the best wine?" And one simply needs to look at just "how tempting dubious blends are". We must all be mindful of the fact, the permanent secretary goes on to emphasize the point, that champagne making "must be monitored and sensitively dealt with by qualified winegrowers" and in order for it to be profitable they should be dealing with known quantities. They needed to invest in sophisticated equipment, ensuring it is well maintained and replaced as and when required … The rewards reaped by members' work may potentially be seriously affected if they carried on as we are now. It appears that if champagne making by winegrowers is "ardently hoped for" by the Union then success can be attributed to collaboration. And working together means working in a cooperative. The newspaper

1- Henri Macquart had been a key player in the winegrowers' unionist movement. Furthermore, he played an equally dominant role in inter-professional relations and the cooperative movement before launching the impressive Centre Vinicole de la Champagne in the early 1970's.

2- Jean Nollevalle became permanent secretary of the SGVC after the second world war, where he remained for more than thirty years. He was a highly influential figure in the champagne cooperative world.

columns of La Champagne viticole are brimming with enthusiasm: "Aside from potential openings it offers, small scale[31] champagne production will result in greater balance and financial security and will enable the producer to operate outside the confines of routine (sic), giving him greater self-confidence. But the ground must be prepared before selling, and this is when the cooperative plays a decisive role. This gives rise to the potential development of the more powerful cooperatives selling their brand."

But for the present time cooperatives need to focus on making champagne and the individual members on being responsible for achieving their own sales targets.

The winegrowers take their grapes to the pressing machine. This expensive piece of equipment belongs to the buyers. Winegrowers had since the end of the nineteenth century grouped together in order to buy and share the materials they used, which enabled some of them to begin to make their own champagne in very limited quantities.

After the Second World War the Champagne region's output fluctuated, a pattern that had been repeated before, with some years characterised by overproduction, others by stagnation. It is important to remember that this instability affected both buyer and winegrower. Winegrowers and traders engaged in tentative dialogues within the context of the inter-professional bodies set up. A global contract managing the grape market signed by both parties could regulate by common consent the champagne economy and promote a policy of expansion and development. But it wasn't until 1959 that the first inter-professional

31. This adjective was chosen by the editor who clearly wished to moderate his language, and is in contradiction with the scope of the project outlined in the sentence.

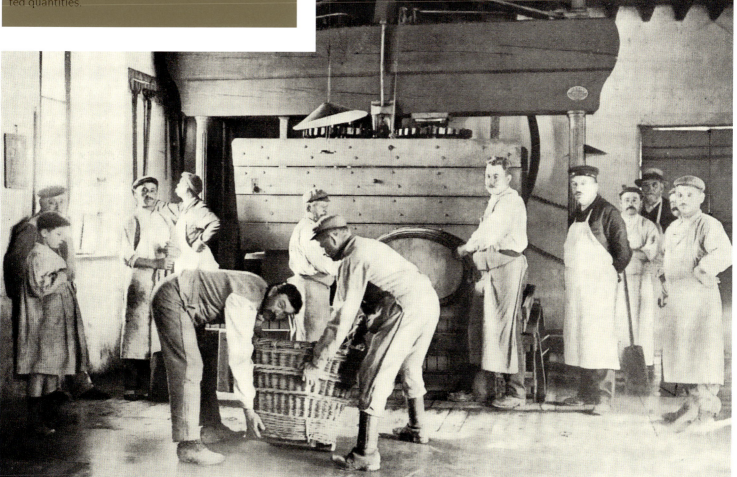

contract was drawn up and implemented. Much like those that were to follow, the aims of the contract were to facilitate sales of the producers' grapes and pave the way for buyers to freely purchase the quantities they wanted over several years.

The cooperation continued to play an active role within this innovative context. Not only was it fulfilling its remit to ensure storage space facilities were adequate, it was also making champagne and researching into technology in a bid to raise the quality of champagne. Moreover, the range of stock justified this highly technical set up which was to improve not only the quality of wines but also their availability on the market. Furthermore, the diversity of stocks justified their blending. This latest development was to open up new and hitherto unexplored horizons. Business was clearly on an upward trend, so much so that by 1968, just ten years later, the brands produced by 24 cooperatives sold 2,750,000 bottles, which accounted for 3% of the total market share for the year.

Restructurisation called for greater solidarity amongst winegrowers and a reorganization of the various groups. It was at this time that the champagne industry saw the emergence of cooperatives set up at regional level and a merging of individual cooperatives, justifying once again the old adage: "Together we are stronger." Winegrowers were not always aware of the radical changes taking place, yet the development of these powerful bodies was impinging upon the balance of power of the buyers who since the 1960's had carved a powerful niche for themselves.

This is how the CRVC in Reims, the Union Champagne at Mesnil-sur-Oger and the Union Auboise at Bar-sur-Seine were formed at the time of the bumper harvest of 1970.

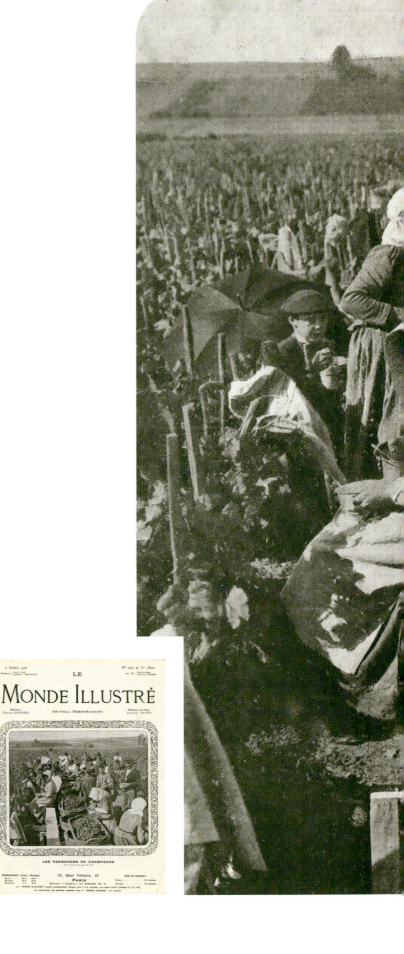

1

1 - 2. Featured in an article of the 17th October 1909 edition of the weekly paper *Le Monde illustré*, these superb quality photos depict several scenes of the 1909 harvest. On the previous page, the women grape pickers, at work in the vineyards and protected from the sun by their "bavolet" the regional hat wear typical of the era which had a protective back flap, hand-pick their grapes by grading the bunches and fruit and place them in willow baskets before being dispatched to the pressing machine. Below, the often very young grape-pickers, leave the vineyard at the end of the day singing in chorus.

After the exceptional harvest of 1970, a group of enterprising producers supporting Henri Macquart, the President of the Fédération des coopératives vinicoles de Champagne, began thinking about an innovative facility that still today is one of its kind: the Centre Vinicole de la Champagne, the precursor of the Centre Vinicole – Champagne Nicolas Feuillatte.

The Foundation

1970. From the end of September to mid October, a group of grape pickers toiled from dawn till dusk for a daily sum of 34 francs[32], harvesting some 250,000 tons of grapes. A yield of this level was unheard of in the Champagne region[33]! The presses were working flat out and some 800,000 barrels of wine (producing 164,000,000 litres) were made with a phenomenal number of bunches of grapes. This was an exceptional result when compared with the average 330,000 barrels produced in the two preceding years. Professionals were ill-prepared for this exceptionally fruitful harvest. They monitored the way the vines grew for several weeks. Despite counting all the vats, barrels and a few old dusted big wooden vats, the winegrowers, traders and cooperative members could see that existing storage facilities were totally inadequate. So, some of the producers remembered the canal boats that in years gone by were used to transport wine along rivers and canals and in that Autumn of 1970 some of the quays of Marne were used over a period of a few weeks in the transportation of wine. It's always worth taking a risk, so long as it leads to a solution, albeit a temporary one. Indeed some of the larger reservoirs that had fallen into disuse were restored and temporarily refreshed with a liquid they'd never been filled with before ...

"The reservoir at Damery is the one everyone remembers, were there others? I couldn't tell you, says Jean-Pierre Daraut, the man at the helm of the CIVC today[34], but it's important to remember what happened. One thing is for sure that barrels were being bought left, right and centre. Everyone was in a state of panic[35]! And the following Spring the wines smelled of port, brandy and whisky ..."

In fact it was an incredible year. People were working flat out with the pressing equipment. Every single mode of transport was requisitioned and the excitement engendered by this exceptional harvest was equalled by a deep felt concern for the potential losses it in could incur. All things considered, this extraordinary yield (13,800 kg/ha) has to date never been equalled[36]. The only year that has ever come close to it was 1973, (11,750 kg/ha[37]) by which time Champagne had no transportation, grape pressing and most significantly storage issues to contend with. There was no need to requisition canal boats or indeed reservoirs as much work had been done to improve the available facilities and equipment. The harvests of 1971 and 1972 had

---

32. The equivalent today is approximately 34 euros.
33. The total surface of the production area was 17,888 hectares in 1970.
34. Jean-Pierre Daraut, born in Barzy (Aisne) near Château-Thierry in 1938 had by 1970 been the engineer advising the Comité interprofessionnel de vin de Champagne on technical matters for four years.
35. Even the Olympic sized swimming pool at Reims built in 1967 had been considered as a provisional reservoir. The instigators had not thought it bizarrely out of the question. Yet the idea was abandoned because of conservation issues.
36. This figure should be read in relation to the production surface area. The figure was surpassed several times over as the appellation area grew.
37. More precisely 11,221 kg according to the archives of the Centre Vinicole de la Champagne.

brought some respite; 1971, a low water year, saw 5,100 kg of grapes harvested per hectare. In order to find a yield lower than that, one has to go as far back as 1958 when 4,800 kg were harvested per hectare. 1972, plagued by a low rainfall and cool summer, was only marginally better, but the harvest was a catastrophe, with 9,000 kg[38] of unripe grapes agonizingly harvested per hectare.

Yet these setbacks had little impact on the decade's average yield. Between 1970 and 1979, the stock level was 91% higher than the preceding decade. Even so, it is worth comparing these figures with the average number of hectares cultivated specifically for champagne in the 60's and 70's: 14,238 hectares in the decade 1960-1969 and 21,267 in 1970-1979. A handful of prescient producers had foreseen this exponential growth, yet what they had to say fell on deaf ears. Everyone did however stand up and take notice when faced with the profusion of grapes and a region-wide dearth of equipment in 1970. In a bid to deal with the imminent consequences and overcome the issue of a lack of mechanical equipment, both winegrowers and buyers increased the number of grape pressers and enlarged their tank halls over the following months. If the situation for cooperatives is the same, then they share a cultural heritage that equips them to deal with the future with greater confidence.

This time, the union that dealt with the situation in the most effective way bypassed the weaker framework of the cooperative which had limited powers. A group of enterprising producers and supporters of Henri Macquart, the President of Syndicat des vignerons up until 1960 and President at the Fédération des coopératives vinicoles de Champagne since 1946, went on to found the Centre Vinicole de laChampagne[39], the first and only to date storage and vinification unit of its

---

38. Exactly 8,867 kg according to the archived paperwork of the CVC.
39. At the extraordinary general meeting held on 22 July 1972, the CVC was to become the CVC Union des coopératives agricoles with the application of Article 46 of 4th February 1959. But as far as everyone is concerned, the Centre Vinicole de la Champagne is called the CVC, or the Centre, or indeed the Super Coop.

1891-1893
The first cooperative set up by René Lamarre in Damery (51).
1904
The setting up of the Fédération des vignerons.
1911
Champagne winegrowers rebelling against fraudulent practices.
1919
The Syndicat général des vignerons de la Champagne (SGVC) follows on from the Fédération des vignerons.
1921
COGEVI, the first Champagne cooperative set up in Dizy.
1927
The Indépendante de Festigny cooperative, set up by Marcel Berthelot.
1939
Marcel Berthelot sets up the Fédération des coopératives vinicoles de la Champagne on 3rd June.
1941
12th April, setting up of the Comité interprofessionnel du vin de Champagne (CIVC), the joint organization, co-chaired by a buyers' representative and winegrowers' representative.
1959
The institution of the first inter-professional contract.
1972
The founding of the Centre Vinicole de la Champagne (CVC), the cooperative union chaired by Henri Macquart.
1978
The official inauguration of the CVC on 7th July.
1986
On 6th March the Nicolas Feuillatte brand is acquired by the CVC.
2001
The CVC becomes the Centre Vinicole – Champagne Nicolas Feuillatte (CV-CNF).

MAP OF THE CHAMPAGNE REGION

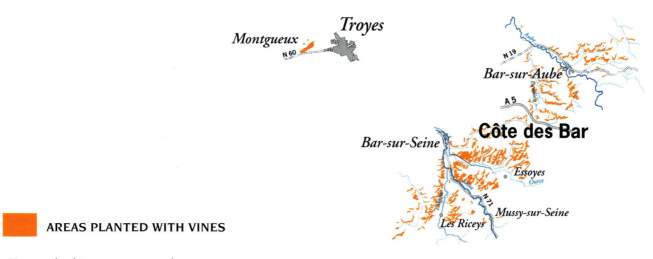

■ AREAS PLANTED WITH VINES

Verzy The biggest town in the canton

Henri Macquart

The founder. Henri Macquart (1914-2005) dreamt up the Centre Vinicole and turned it into reality. After having worked at the Centre from 1972 to 1981 he was appointed Chairman of the Board of Directors, a position he held until 1997. Henri Macquart saw his project materialize and witnessed the enterprise he had set up grow in tandem with the evolving needs of his winegrowers. His charisma was infectious, and felt by all his contemporaries, and as a man who knew all there was to know about winegrowing he was dependable, sensible, wise, and full of good will, qualities that were valued by colleagues. Committed to the unionist cause from early on in his career (he was president of the Syndicat des Vignerons until 1960 and elected president of the Fédération des coopératives vinicoles de la Champagne in 1946), he gained the respect of the whole of the profession and was able to overcome the divisions in the aftermath of the war whilst upholding his convictions. He was without question one of the principal actors in the champagne industry.

kind, which was later to become the Centre Vinicole – Champagne Nicolas Feuillatte in 2001. It would be impossible to turn this bold initiative into a success without significant financial support and what level of resources could a handful of producers rallying together possibly amass? In order to raise sufficient funds, the cooperatives had to unite, be persuaded of the viability of the project and most importantly be made aware of the potential financial advantages an enterprise of this kind could provide. In less than two years this is what Henri Macquart and his associates set about to achieve. They held meeting after meeting in a bid to convince other cooperative members in the Champagne region of the benefits of uniting to form a buoyant organisation which they could belong to without having to renounce their independence. Yet the significant quota each member was asked to contribute would not give him sole use of the storage and vinification facilities to which he would have access.

"Monsieur Macquart explained the project thoroughly" said André Patis, the champagne producer who in 1970 was Treasurer of the Œuilly cooperative in Marne. Like so many others, he had been elected by his peers, and subsequently appointed by neighbouring cooperatives which led to him representing them at board meetings. If discussions ran smoothly, and the official from the outset was pleased to note, it was because of the "calm atmosphere and spirit of cooperation" in which they were held. According to one participant "Discussions were firm and money was the main agenda. Monsieur Macquart remained unperturbed as he listened to the various mediators". Jean Deliège[40], a former Vice-president of the Centre concurs. "Somewhat taciturn yet sure of himself Henri Macquart conducted himself impeccably throughout the proceedings. He was not once contentious with either the producers or the buyers. For example he showed no hesitation in saying to the buyers "It is absurd that the Champagne region lacks the storage facilities to cater for abundant harvests. We shall overcome this hurdle that was previously impossible to deal with …" A second priority for the CVC president was to find a suitable location for the future Centre. He delegated the matter to Jean-Pierre Daraut, the recently elected Director[41]. "Ambonnay was the preferred choice for the proposed site, but the sale of the land fell through at the eleventh hour. Besides we needed a minimum of five hectares. We finally decided upon Chouilly as it offered us the greatest amount of space[42]". This site offered several advantages to the initiators of the Centre. Besides it being potentially extendible, it was strategically located in the symbolic heart of the Champagne region opposite Montagne de Reims and Côte des Blancs, dominating the Vallée de la Marne between Épernay and Châlons-en-Champagne and en route towards Sézannais and Aube.

1971. A succession of meetings was held in 1971. The sale of the land went through and the first members' meeting was held in Épernay on 7th August later that year.

That morning the producers, each sent by their Board of Directors and representing some 40 cooperatives in the Champagne region, gathered in Épernay, at the headquarters of the Fédération des Coopératives vinicoles de la Champagne (FCVC)[43]. They hailed from Ambonnay, Aÿ, Baslieux-sous-Châtillon, Boursault, Châtillon-sur-Marne, Chaumuzy, Chigny-les-Roses, Cuis, Étoges, Ferbrianges, Festigny, Fleury-la-Rivière, Jouy-les-Reims, Grauves, Montigny-sous-Châtillon, Moussy, Nesle-le-Repons, Œuilly, Passy-Grigny, Passy-sur-Marne, Pierry, Pouillon, Reuil, Rilly-la-Montagne,

---

40. Jean Deliège was born in 1928. By this stage he was one of Henri Macquart's right-hand men and was therefore one of the pioneers of the CVC.
41. Jean-Pierre Daraut was hoping to leave the CIVC. Upon hearing about the Centre Vinicole project he applied for a position to work alongside Henri Macquart. The president appointed the engineer and oenologist as a Director after a brief interview. From then on, he was part of the new project and one of its main protagonists between 1972 and 1993.
42. In fact, in the early days the CVC had bought only one and a half hectares, but there were enormous potential to purchase more land. The CVC acquired much more land which meant that the CVC was spread over several tens of hectares.
43. At the time, 44 Avenue Jean-Jaurès was also where the headquarters of the Syndicat général des vignerons de Champagne. Today both bodies are located at 17, Avenue de Champagne in Épernay.

Saint-Martin-d'Ablois, Sermiers, Serzy-et-Prin, Trigny, Troissy, Vandeuil, Vandières, Vaudemanges, Venteuil, Verneuil (L'Économe), Verneuil (Saint-Vincent), Villedommange (Société des Producteurs), Villeneuve (UCAVIC), Villevenard (Cave des Dîmes), Villevenard (Les Côteaux de) and Vinay.

After Henri Macquart welcomed the delegates and set out the agenda, Jacques Houdard[44], a lawyer from Épernay, read the statute of the Centre Vinicole de la Champagne. The two main topics discussed at the meeting and recorded in the minutes were the procedures required for appointing members and how they were to be represented in the Centre.

The contribution made by each cooperative depended on the size of their winery. But in order to ensure the Centre's viability a minimum amount of champagne supplies had to met by each member. The way each cooperative was represented was based on its individual contribution, with 1,000 hectolitres guaranteeing them one representative.

Once these two issues had been clearly laid out and debated, the meeting approved its statute unanimously. Then appointments were made to the Board of Governors. Those elected were Norbert Sartoré (Villedommange), Pierre Gillet, (La Neuville-sur-Seine), Roland Rondeau (Jouy-lès-Reims), Maurice Robert (Cuis), André Patis (Œuilly), Guy Lété (Venteuil), James Didier (Brugny-Vaudancourt) and Jean Vatel (Verneuil). Henri Macquart (Pourcy) was automatically re-elected President, André Vandier vice-president (Bethon) and Serge Rafflin Treasurer (Ludes).

Matters were proceeding apace when, the Board having been duly registered, Henri Macquart "explained to the meeting the need to appoint specialists to rigorously investigate and assess the potential for investment". A Paris-based research group, the OCCR Inter G[45] had already been asked to carry out some preliminary research. A global sum of one million two hundred and fifty thousand francs was the estimated amount required for construction works[46]. As for planning "the project will be ready to go and will be fully completed by the builders in time for the 1972 harvest". There was nothing else in the minutes about the construction of the site. The minutes of the extraordinary meeting held in March 1972 were much more specific. In any event, after the discussions held about the "proposed financial outline" it was decided that the research should continue, and the meeting was called to a close at 1.00pm.

Less than eight months later, on 16th March 1972, Henri Macquart called for an extraordinary general meeting of the Centre Vinicole de la Champagne at 3.00pm at the Palais des Fêtes in Épernay. The meeting was packed to the gills with members. Even so, of the 50 cooperatives that had signed up only 45 were represented. Jacques Bertrand, the Chief Executive of Inter G, attended the meeting in person, accompanied by the architect René Baccot. They gave an account of how the research they had been commissioned to undertake was progressing and expounded "with utmost clarity and in great detail" on the specialised research carried out in strict collaboration with a number of technicians from the vineyard, most notably Monsieur Gratadour of COGEVI and Monsieur Maury of the UCAVIC.

A walk-in and three dimensional scaled down model had been built[47] for all those involved to inspect. A selection of plans had been brought to the meeting enabling the members to follow the discussions on the technical information.

As could be seen from the paperwork, the Centre comprised two main and interconnected buildings. A single storey construction, the complex facilitated movement from one site to another of the Centre Vinicole. It was most apparent that the architects had tried their best to respond to the project's technical demands with a modern facility. Over time the Centre

---

44. His son Jean-Louis Houdard took over from him.
45. Initial contact was made with the regional office of Ligat who having been made fully aware of the scope of the project directed the team towards OCCR Inter G.
46. Approximately 2,000,000 euros today.
47. This model has not been kept.

From the end of September to mid-October 1970 the grape pickers work tirelessly as 250,000 tons of grapes need to be harvested.

Part one - A unique story | PAGE 33

Vinicole – Champagne Nicolas Feuillatte developed organically around this central nucleus, which is just what the founders had hoped for. The builders that followed had to preserve this highly rational complex, and this was central to the success of the Centre Vinicole.

The cuverie was clearly regarded as the complex's focal point, and it was the vinification unit so longed for by the champagne producers. It was divided into three sections each with a capacity of 10,000 hectolitres[48] housing 1,000, 200 and 100 hectolitre tanks. The set up of the cuvée and second press was also specified at the meeting. The vat hall was to be refrigerated by a stream of icy cold running water to maintain the temperature at 18° C, thus ensuring that the wines' characteristics would remain intact for an optimum production. "We also added 4,000 hectolitres capacity temperature controlled tanks to the 30,000 hectolitres capacity tanks where the wine underwent cold treatment after blending" our enthused chronicler recounts[49]. Furthermore, "The tanks were all made with stainless steel and conformed to the highest standards of quality", additional proof of everyone's eagerness to create a highly efficient and modern facility.

Today, those running the Centre can see that the optimisation of production was a priority for the founders of the Centre Vinicole. Since the beginning this enterprising group of men knew from the very outset that building efficient storage space was just one phase in the project. One harvest follows on from the next and tanks have to be ready for the next batch. The bottles were piling up in the cellar and more space needed to be built quickly.

Since March 1973 the Director had made plans "to house 12,000 barrels in the recently finished tank hall". If at all feasible, the complex had to be enlarged, and this has been a major concern for those running the Centre. Investing time and effort in producing a quality wine was another. The multi-faceted roles performed by different sized tanks was indicative of the Directors desire to produce the wine in the best possible way and this was achieved by separating the must according to qualitative criteria[50] that took into account the provenance of the grapes. Furthermore, "quality control mechanisms were in place the moment the must arrived in the hall, and each batch, depending on its provenance, was designated to a particular section of the cuverie".

Best of all, the laboratory is equipped with machinery that can perform an automatic analysis of the grape must. The examinations, taking minutes to complete, prevent any disastrous blends from being made in addition to treating must whose properties have been subject to alteration by pre-fermentary cold stabulation. A short while later an annexed laboratory as is built to analyse "the samples provided quickly and at no cost to the producer". The construction of this laboratory was further proof of the invaluable service it provided in the Champagne region.

The technical hub at the heart of the operation controlled every piece of equipment needed in the vinification process. It also contained a dedicated enclosed area for preparing yeast, and this was something that had never been seen in the region before.

"Jacques Bertrand had previously worked in a brewery and he knew all about yeast[51]", recounts Jean-Pierre Daraut. Under his guidance we grew yeast in continuous culture and at high concentrations. So we installed an automatic fermenter". It is the only one of its kind in the region and is still used today.

Still a project in the making are halls designated for making and blending liqueurs, a stabulation chamber equipped with filtering apparatus and a bottling line.

For the time being, the office space may well be very limited, but the cellars are enormous. There are no old quarries to be transformed at Chouilly and as one of the principle aims of the site is to facilitate internal transferral, further excavation of the cellars is out of the question. Some detached modular buildings are therefore constructed at

---

48. In 1971 the total storage capacity for all the cooperatives was "20,000 hectolitres", according to André Garcia, PUF in *Les Vins de Champagne*.
49. This account is given by Jean-Pierre Daraut.
50. These separated vinification processes had already been adopted in the region, but without equipment of this level.
51. Yeast is an essential component of the fermentation process, as without it the results achieved can be arbitrary.

ground level. A concept on this scale and in this region is nothing short of revolutionary. The refrigeration plant and heating system come into their own in order to maintain the ambient temperature at 11/12 ° C. Inter G had big ideas; bottles could be stored in crates, stacked on four levels in a new-look cellar and the empty bottles stacked in a separate designated area planned for outside the buildings.

There's not much time left to build this vast complex between March 1973 and the next harvest. The members are acutely aware of this and led by President Macquart, they approve the project's final plans and financial strategy drawn up by the study group who are to take charge of the construction of the site. The proposal is unanimously voted in at the general meeting, where the atmosphere is positive when the financial matters are raised. Monsieur Sichère from the Caisse régionale de Crédit Agricole de Reims (CRCA) said that despite "the research undertaken regarding the most favourable financial prospects[52]", it is nevertheless crucially important that the initially approved share capital be significantly increased. Now, it is a well known fact that certain cooperatives have since 1972 had financial management issues. But the word "cooperation" is a weighty term and the CRCA opens a medium-term (three years) credit facility to the cooperatives that wish to increase their supplementary contribution to the Centre's share capital. The enthusiasm visibly waned in the hall.

"Some of the members protested" Jean-Pierre Daraut recalls. They claimed they hadn't a penny left and the project was getting bigger and bigger. Macquart boldly called for a secret ballot. As I handed out the scraps of hastily cut paper which were then placed into a hat belonging to a council member I kept telling myself this is a disaster, a disaster …

The results of the poll were surprising: almost 100% of the voters agree with the proposal to increase the share capital to 130 francs (121 euros today) per hectolitre. A formidable outcome that "demonstrates everyone's desire to proceed with the project whatever the cost". There is one other resolution in the minutes that Henri Macquart hopes is adopted: article 1 of the by-laws concerning the commitment needed to be made by each cooperative to hand over all the stipulated quantities of grape must and pay any penalties if they fail to do so. In short, those breaching the regulations must redeem all loans, pay the staff, contribute to maintenance costs, pay back loans for equipment and pay at a pro rata rate all the costs incurred by the Centre. Everyone agrees to these conditions and after three hours of deliberations and election of the auditors, namely Lucien Paté, the accountant from Reims, Jean-Baptiste Bagnost, a producer from Pierry and Guy Rion, a producer from Courmas, the meeting is adjourned. The existing members are pleased to note the involvement of other cooperatives. Bethon (La Crayère), Champillon, Coulommes-la-Montagne, Olizy-Violaine are most positive about their affiliation to the cooperative.

"It was on this basis" as reported in an internal archived document "that the Centre Vinicole de la Champagne began life. It's abiding objective has been to fulfil the needs of its members, its bona fide founders, and to contribute more and more to the financial security of Champagne."

The desire to succeed and the enthusiasm for the project has remained resolute to this day. There are many who believe more than ever that the future holds radiant times ahead for the cooperative. The organisation flourishes in the years following its inception, but nobody could have foreseen the financial, social and political direction the Centre was to take as a result of the ensuing developments. One thing is for sure: the Centre Vinicole is a cooperative and as shall become apparent later, the decisions, whatever they may be, were always taken with its members' interests at heart.

---

52. This financial potential takes into account the most likely loans given by the CRCA in addition to subsidies given by the state and the CIVC. The subsidies provided by the CIVC are equal to "a quarter of the envisaged expenses", and are of enormous benefit insofar as they significantly reduce each member's contribution. Regrettably the level of financial aid expected to be given by the CIVC was nowhere near what it should have been. Therefore at the general meeting of 8th March 1973 president Macquart voiced his concerns and told his members that "The CIVC has reneged on its subsidies because of the buyers-winegrowers coalition".

1 - 2 - 3. In the Spring of 1972 the bulldozers and concrete mixers work non stop. The pre-stressed concrete girders providing the supportive structure to the buildings, which were highly innovative at the time, and partition walls are erected. As the building begins to take shape, this modern construction looks like a "château made from playing cards", a nickname chosen by its critics.

The building work

In May 1972 the film directed by Claude Lelouch, *L'Aventure c'est l'aventure*, appeared on cinema screens throughout France. But for the champagne producers of the CVC, keen to get a grip on the future, there's nothing remotely exotic about the Chouilly project.

Whatever the costs involved are, their ambitious project is developing well, with all the administrative and commercial (sale, exchange, registration etc.) hurdles overcome. The more impatient members are reassured by the construction work taking place on the site.

The bulldozers and concrete mixers work non stop. The construction company Thouraud de Cormicy is contracted to make the pre-stressed concrete girders providing the supportive structure to the buildings[53], in addition to the partition walls. As the building begins to take shape, this modern construction looks like a "château made from playing cards", a nickname given by its critics.

At this point in time weekly meetings are held on the site; the managers, president and the director in particular are keen to involve other cooperatives in the project. The target of 30,000 hectolitres of stock in preparation for the following harvest has not been reached, and it is essential it is achieved as without it the Centre will fall into a backlog of reneged repayments.

53. This was at the time a ground breaking technique.

"I picked up my pilgrim's staff" recalls Jean-Pierre Daraut, "and went to see the cooperatives in Marne, Aisne and Aube. I talked to them about what was at stake and tried to convince them of the benefits of belonging to the organisation. The meetings were held in the evening as everyone was at work during the day. I returned home late at night, feeling either frustrated or elated. On one happy occasion, I remember returning home triumphantly telling everyone I'd achieved a 250-300 hecto target[54]."

One cooperative after another signed up, and the target was almost reached in June. At the ordinary general meeting held on 22 July the director announced that most of the work had been done and that the vat hall was taking shape. Two of the three modules had been installed. 6,000,000 francs[55] had already been spent and as long as there would be no further unexpected costs, the cooperative would be shortly up and running and in a position to house grape must stocks within the desired time frame. The architect overseeing the project and his team had performed fantastically well. The harvest was going to proceed according to plan.

Aside from the construction of the buildings, the Centre assures all its members that it will take responsibility for the transportation of the grape must in addition to organising the delivery of the bottled wines to the cooperatives.

"I would like to make it clear to all members that these procedures will promote full traceability of intake and guarantee the finest quality Champagne." It would also avoid the potential chaos of unchecked transportation. Wasn't it Aeschylus that said obedience was the mother of success[56]?

On 1st September 1972 the Centre was staffed by 7 permanent employees. Jean-Pierre Daraut is in charge of the recruitment of staff, and it proves to be a difficult task as people are reluctant to make the commute to the Centre. He fails to appoint a Secretary and ends up by asking his father-in-law to fill the position temporarily.

54. A hectolitre was a unit of measurement that corresponded to each member's share.
55. Slightly more than 900,000 euros today.
56. Aeschylus, Greek poet (525 - 456 AC), in The Seven against Thebes.

1 - 2. Contrast between the vineyard and concrete. As the bunches of grapes ripen, the buildings emerge from the ground. Everything has got to be ready for the 1972 harvest. It is a race against time for the Centre's president and team. The outcome remains unclear until October.

"Most importantly the first position I had to fill was the cellar master. I purloined Jacky Gaunel who was at the time working for the Vincelles Cooperative which had not at that point in time affiliated itself with the Centre[57]. An upright sort of fellow, he knew everything there was to know about winemaking and I trusted his taste implicitly."

André Welche then joined Chouilly as the key contact dealing with the winegrowers. He knew all things agricultural, and managed and later directed the public relations department up until December 1995. The only woman in the male dominated team was the highly capable Yvonne Virey who ran the laboratory. The maintenance of a mass of machinery and pipe work (including an air conditioning unit that was in operation at all times) needed to be supervised by a head technician, namely Jacques Hocquier who had previously worked at Virax, a company based in Épernay specialising in the manufacture of professional equipment. The other two members of this small team were Jean-Marie Rion, who fulfilled a variety of roles[58] and Marcel Durand, chief security officer and his dogs. It was at the general meeting of July 1972 during the course of which the inventory was discussed, that Henri Macquart, keen to personally inform each member present and hear their opinions and suggestions, asked the president of each cooperative to provide a list of their members in order to address them individually through an industry journal[59].

This journal was to complement the pioneers' painstaking efforts in getting the project off the ground. The results were clear to see: the Centre Vinicole had a membership of 53 cooperatives and subsequently it was they that took the bull by the horns, urging others to join the group. This sort of publicity did not simply attract the attention of other cooperatives and their leaders. Word had got round very early on and it was only natural that the Centre Vinicole was approached by individual producers who were not affiliated to any cooperative[60].

57. The Vincelles Cooperative joined the CVC in 1988.
58. Jean-Marie Rion is only one of the Centre's pioneers to be working at the CVC in 2010.
59. In fact, the first edition of the journal was instigated by Dominique Pierre and published in 1995.
60. It was impossible for independent winegrowers to join the CVC as they had to previously be affiliated to a regional cooperative that had itself to belong to the CVC and had to adhere to CVC's regulations.

There are no old quarries to be transformed at Chouilly and further excavation of the cellars is out of the question. Some detached modular buildings are therefore constructed at ground level. A concept on this scale and in this region is nothing short of revolutionary.

"I was approached very early on by a champagne maker from Vertus, Jean-Marie Thomas. He was aware of what we were doing and was duly impressed". Jean-Pierre Daraut adds "He believed that enlargement would lead to bigger and better things."

Yet he was entirely independent and the cooperative's statute precluded the involvement of individual producers. Nevertheless, this did not deter others from making approaches. André Welche[61] later took charge of the initiative and formed an association run along similar lines to a cooperative which individual producers could join. "They joined an arm of COGEVI specifically for independent producers." But the number of those joining was so great that the Aÿ cooperative could no longer cope so they requested to join the CVC. Their demands were met and in February 1974 the UPPCVC was formed[62]. "Setting up the UPPCVC was one of the best things we ever did", the enthused former director general recounts. In attracting a growing membership the union went on to play an important role in the history of the Centre Vinicole de la Champagne, giving it increasing credibility.

No-one at the time held great hopes for the harvest of 1972 due to the unfavourable weather conditions that had swept across the Champagne region. Indeed it was nothing short of catastrophic, the wines produced in that year were unmemorable.

"1972 was the worst year I've ever known", recalls Jean-Pierre Daraut who, like everyone at the CVC, had harboured high hopes for their first year. The potential

61. André Welche, initially the key person liaising with the winegrowers, was later promoted to the position of Director of Public Relations, a position he held until his departure from the Centre at the end of 1995.
62. UPPCVC is the acronym for Union des propriétaires particuliers du Centre Vinicole de la Champagne.
63. Seven degrees corresponding to a potential 7% alcohol by volume content which could be transformed into residual sugars. An average of 10 degrees is regarded as promising in the region and corresponds (after fermentation) to 170 grams of residual sugars per litre.

alcohol content had reached an all time low of 7°C[63], and for many around 5 and 6°C"!

But the worst was yet to come. A fire broke out in mid September in one of the site's buildings as work was in progress in the tank hall just when the director was asking himself how could they pick the majority of the pathetically unripe grapes. "The inept deployment of a blowtorch set fire to the polyurethane in a partition wall", a fuming Jean-Pierre Daraut explains, who had been on site to oversee the final and crucially important touches being added to the hall." The fire spread quickly to the other plastic layers on the hall's double partitions. This disastrous fire spread to the second tank hall which was at the time geared up to handling the imminent arrival of the grape must. There were a handful of people on site but they were unable to deal with the onslaught of smoke "which rose two metres above the site". It took several hours before the fire fighters were able to extinguish the flames. When at long last they gained entry into the two halls, the effects had been devastating.

"There was no damage done to the stainless steel tanks," recalls Jean-Pierre Daraut with tears in his eyes, "but they were covered in a several millimetre thick layer of greasy soot …", as was the pipe work, all the surfaces, floors and walls. Macquart tried to console his members: "We will not be defeated! Every company I've set up has had a fire at the beginning. And things turned out for the better. Keep your spirits up!"

But the team's spirits are at an all time low. They feel disconsolate but time is running out. A flicker or two of hope emerges, with some members believing that despite everything, the harvested grapes can be collected. At first, faced with the pitiful condition of the grapes, the secateurs are put to use as late as 10th October, as decreed by the powers that be[64]. This two-week delay does not bode well for the quality of the grapes, but it is most welcome, given the circumstances.

And, as witnessed by everyone, the tanks, in a correctly cleaned condition, will perform extremely well, and it is René Baccot, the project manager, who makes this task his priority[65]. "He took the bull by the horns" and engaged the services of a company based in Paris specialising in this type of cleaning. With a daily commute between the capital and Chouilly and equipped with materials for the job, the cleaning staff worked round the clock for two weeks to get the job finished.

The construction workers in the meantime finished with great speed the third module of the tank hall. "Remotivating the crew was no small achievement", concludes Jean-Pierre Daraut, "but we got there." Two weeks later all traces of soot damage had practically disappeared and the first batch of grape must could be delivered.

Something had to be done with the 25,000 hectolitres of wine that everyone knew was from the worst harvest ever seen in the second half of the twentieth century. The Centre could not rely on vins de réserve to improve subsequent blends.

"Each cooperative jealously guarded their supplies. Only two of them were given permission to give us a few hectolitres, amounting to a miserable 340 hectolitres in total." The director had to enlist the support of everyone he knew in the industry "in order to get something out of these miserable supplies"!

He used as much sugar as was legally permitted, and in an unprecedented move, added some spirit of cognac[66] purchased as an emergency measure and with the recently reconditioned equipment fermented the wine at a very low temperature. "But not low enough for the fermentation process to cease working …", he muses.

64. The harvest dates were fixed every year by prefectoral by laws (the regional governors relied upon advice given to them by an observational network [the réseau matu], set up in 1956. There were escape clauses pertaining to the agreement which depended on the age of the individual's vineyards.
65. Following on from this disaster, a firm relationship developed between Jean-Pierre Daraut and René Baccot. "The site meant everything to me", the project manager confided some forty years later.
66. This addition of grape alcohol is added to increase the overall alcohol potential.

When it came to bottling the wines early the following year "it did to all intents and purposes look like wine. It had a bouquet, and much to everyone's relief, we bottled it in March. At the end of the day, we'd managed to produce a champagne that, when tasted, was actually better than many others bottled by other cooperatives".

This comparison was undoubtedly favourable and stood the Centre in good stead, particularly when it came to encouraging renewed membership the following year. In 1973 the Centre Vinicole de la Champagne doubled its share capital and by its second harvest had processed 50,000 hectolitres of grape must. Jean Deliège finds it astonishing still today. "I was surprised to see a number of the cooperatives renew their membership. It was just like when the independent producers were so keen to join. I couldn't believe it."

The members had good cause to feel satisfied at the general meeting held on 8th March 1973, starting with their first harvests which despite the winds and floods had turned out well in their recently completed vat hall. The staff are in buoyant mood and are thanked for their work accomplished in the face of adversity. A bottling line is fully operational by the Spring which meant that approximately 20,000 hectolitres of the 25,000 hectolitres received could be bottled[67]. "At the beginning of the project" recalls Jean-Pierre Daraut "we were settled on the idea of constructing just a winery, but shortly afterwards we also built cellars because if we were not in a position to sell the wine made at the first harvest we would have had to bottle and store it." It is worth bearing in mind that very early on that the "bottles earmarked for the members[68]" were only the finished product. The wine that had been partially finished[69] had to be monitored by the Centre to guarantee maximum profit from buoyant markets, taking into account the storage capacity which was soon to prove to be very limited.

The following four years were characterised by steady development, consolidation of the measures that had been taken, and a concerted desire to ease oral communication across the board. Since February 1974, the year affected by the petrol crisis which led to the first worldwide economic crisis in the post second world war period, the board of directors had asked their members "to be the spokesmen for the Centre Vinicole de la Champagne between traders and producers". The Centre's precise role and purpose needed to be clearly stipulated to everyone involved in the production of champagne. The sole aim of the Centre was to serve the interests of each and every member, achievable by taking certain measures, and this holds true still today. This invitation to encourage dialogue supported by Henri Macquart and his friends is a bid to move away from the culture of "unproductive and entrenched positions" taken by the parties involved. The producers remember well the days not so long ago, when with or without a contract, the great champagne houses were calling the shots, having unfair bargaining power over the producers selling their grapes to them. Their mistrust, having been passed from generation to generation, was well and truly engrained. For the most part traders are happy to settle on established positions when it comes to supplies, with yearly renewable contracts signed with the producers. They maintain a somewhat closed mentality and the mutterings amongst the ranks are of no concern to them whatsoever.

"Traders were not in the slightest bit interested in buying our wine" recalls Jean-Pierre Daraut, but we knew that one day the champagne houses would come to us."

It's always easy being right thirty years later. However the visible signs were soon to become apparent to

---

67. This equates to a little under 3,000,000 bottles.
68. The members' could be in effect paid in quotas of corked and labelled bottles that had had sugar added to them. In the early days the bottles the Centre laid down in its cellars had not been earmarked for the members. They were sold as the Centre had to maintain its competitiveness on the market.
69. The French term "vins sur lattes" are bottles that have been nearly finished that buyers, cooperatives or winegrowers then sell to another buyer, cooperative or winegrower. Once the buyer has disgorged the wine and added the sugar he can put his own label on the bottle and then place the bottle on the market.

the vigilant observer. The consumption of champagne was increasing and as the production area expanded so did its Appellation d'Origine Contrôlée (which was reaching its limit). No champagne house is self-sufficient when it comes to grapes, they all, to a greater or lesser extent, rely upon supplies given to them by the producers. It was then that the Centre, set up as a direct consequence of the cooperative movement, but necessarily having to raise its game and increase its power, hoped to play a new role in the industry. What was to stop him from being negotiator capable of easing tensions by offering a credible alternative that could work for the common good and its development? When he sent his members to negotiate between the winegrowers and traders, the president of the CVC saw beyond the habitual squabbling over the vines[70]. "You always knew that Henri Macquart had his head screwed on properly and everything he said turned out to be the case", testifies Jean Deliège who takes pleasure in citing the following proverb: "Hunger brings the wolf out of the wood." In short, he implies that in the event of a poor harvest the traders will have to buy their supplies from where the stocks are healthiest, in other words, from the cellars of the CVC. Meanwhile, avenues, at times bizarre, that could not have been foreseen, mapped out the future development of the profession. The convoluted route taken by 50,000 bottles of the Centre Vinicole till their arrival at the cellars of one of the great champagne houses is an amusing example. Despite our boxes being marked with the acronym CVC, the buyer could not make out the name Centre Vinicole de la Champagne written after these letters." One of the local cooperative's whose name began with C was the Coopérative Vinicole de Chigny-les-Roses, who happened to be one of this house's suppliers. "Our bottles, once rejected by the trader, were deposited at the aforementioned village. Nobody could make neither head nor tail of the situation" an amused Jean-Pierre Daraut recounts "and their head winemaker does not believe to this day that the champagne was made with the grapes harvested in 1972." Of course, this is told a long time after it happened but it does highlight the absurdity of an impasse. It led to president Henri Macquart and one of the leading traders, Bertrand Mure[71], to meet shortly afterwards. It was at this meeting held in Épernay in the Orangerie of Moët & Chandon, vice-president Deliège recalls that "Communication between traders and producers was very tense."

But as they met on several occasions, occasionally at the CIVC headquarters, their mutual respect as they got to know each other better grew. Henri Macquart let Bertrand Mure do all the talking, as he had never been particularly loquacious. Towards the end of the meeting Mure informed Macquart of his intention to buy wines that needed disgorging and labelling. Upon hearing the pronouncement, our president did not turn a hair, acquiesced and, much to my surprise, asked for a rather high price. The deal was done, and the bottles paid for up front and in cash. Not long afterwards we signed a contract with Mercier." Jean-Pierre Daraut concurs "We've always acted reasonably and been open to negotiations with buyers."

Within a few years it had become clear to members that wines that needed to be disgorged and labelled could be sold much more easily by the Centre, and it was imperative to boost sales as stocks were mounting, adding to the fact that harvests are sometimes very good, with the exception of 1974, which was a disastrous year. "We were pressing as much earth as we were grapes. It was heartbreaking." Happily for Jean-Pierre Daraut, 1973 had been a great year and "The Centre had proved its worth, producing high quality wines in this bumper year, more so than it did in its first year of operation." The news was good on the cellar spreadsheets. The 1975 wines are rated as exceptional. 1976 was characterised by low rainfall, but

70. Here the author uses the world galipes, which is the word used in the Champagne region for vines.
71. Betrand Mure (1914 - 2009), president of Moët & Chandon, Mercier and Ruinart.

compensated by a healthy crop of grapes with a high degree of maturity (with an alcoholic potential of 10 to 12 degrees, possibly higher), resulting in rounded, velvety wines of character and structure. The delicate and refined wines of 1977 blend beautifully with the vins de réserve of the year before. The wines of 1978 are full bodied, fresh and fruited, and the decade finishes on a high with the superb vintage of 1979.

All's well at the site: the sixth and seventh cellars are completed in 1977 and work proceeds apace on three new cellars, but the question everyone is asking themselves is what is going to happen to the ever increasing stocks? Some of the bottles will be boxed up in the members' "Retirement Case[72]", and between 10% and 20% of the stock is made up of vins de réserve. "We had to sort this issue out pretty quickly. The "vins sur lattes" can't be kept forever; once it reaches a certain point of development it must be drunk." Which means sold. There is a contingency in tacit agreement with the Director, but nobody dares talk about a marketing strategy. The issue does not interfere with the Centre's expansion. Money continues to be invested and a riddling platform and cold filtering unit are built to improve the production flow. The first bottles are disgorged at the CVC in December. However, the rendement de base (the maximum authorized yield) for AOC Champagne has since 1974 been set at 10,400 kg per hectare, plus a 25% margin equating to 13,000 kg. This reduced production level does not however present the Centre with any significant problems, given that its supplies come from some sixty seven cooperatives spread throughout the Champagne region. Each year of this decade reaps rewards for the members whose commitment[73] is unwavering and it is with much jubilation that the Centre Vinicole de la Champagne is officially inaugurated on 7th July 1978.

As Bernard Hinault is heading for his first victory at the Tour de France, the Centre Vinicole's work comes full circle. Everyone involved in setting up this impressive initiative has good reason to give themselves a pat on the back. The Centre has proved its worth to the whole of the profession. After a guided tour of the buildings, the one thousand or so invitees (members and guests) sat down to what was a memorable banquet held in the riddling hall. What more fitting a tribute could have been held to celebrate the years of hard work and the efficiency and success of this state of the art facility. And how better could they congratulate one another on having achieved unprecedented success? Conversation at the table is lively and for the most part focuses on the long path everyone's taken. Also discussed is what the future holds for the Champagne region in general, inter-professional collaboration options and the exciting times ahead, trends and what could unfold from a budding spirit of cooperation enjoyed by the members. The new unions and cooperatives emerging since the early days the CVC had become increasingly proficient, taking concerted measures to improve the quality of the champagnes produced in their cellars. Little by little, the idea of developing an effective marketing strategy takes seed and was soon to be tentatively touched upon as not everyone, including the most forward thinking members, is ready. At the back of everyone's mind are the fundamental precepts of cooperation: storage and servicing the needs of the industry. And that's all there was to it. This does not deter some cooperatives from developing their own marketing strategy, in addition to selling to buyers and serving the needs of their members. Yet attempts to produce their own brands do not negatively affect the unionist spirit as they are not considered to be central to their activities.

It is with an eye on potential marketing activities that the seventies draw to a close. The concrete mixers are a familiar sight at the Centre Vinicole de la Champagne which by 1979 proudly boasts a membership of 68

72. Once the members have sent their bottles to the cooperative they have the option of reclaiming them and selling them in their retirement. This is a way of increasing their official pension.
73. The funding is set at a fixed price by the Centre "and according to the number of bottles made" once the cost price has been calculated. The sum was not increased for ten years.

On 7th July 1978, the day the Centre is officially inaugurated, a bottle of champagne is smashed against the front elevation of the Centre which has managed the last six champagne harvests. Those at the helm have given themselves plenty of leeway to organise the ceremony and just the right amount of time to prove themselves right.

More than 1,500 people attend the celebrations on 7th July 1978, paying tribute to the successful venture set up by its pioneers working together with president Henri Macquart. Those attending are not only, and most importantly, the cooperative members, but also other operators in the Champagne industry some of whom were somewhat taken aback by the sheer size of the new site.

cooperatives! A suite of offices and a large hall, later called the "Panoramic Hall[74]" are built. The site gets bigger with the addition of three more cellars (the ninth, tenth and eleventh). Three further self-contained buildings are erected and a labelling unit is installed. These additions all contribute towards enhancing the Centre's capacity to produce the end product, the finest bottled champagne ready to be launched on the market. Now that production techniques had been mastered, the CVC vigorously sought out new avenues to pursue.

74. Huguette Chavy approved the decoration of the "Panoramic Hall" which was later baptised the hall Henri-Macquart.

Part one - A unique story | PAGE 47

Under the watchful gaze of president Henri Macquart and the director general Jean-Pierre Daraut, the regional governor Jacques Delaunay cuts the tradition tricolour ribbon. Six years after it had started operating, the Centre Vinicole de la Champagne is officially inaugurated.

1 - 2. As the seasons flow, cooperatives continue to join the CVC, thus increasing supplies and giving it access to a greater number of premiers and grands crus from the vineyards of Champagne.

1981. The death penalty is abolished and the TGV makes its virgin trip from Paris to Lyon. "La fête de la musique" is inaugurated for the first time. A number of banks and large companies are nationalised. France elects a new president[75], and so too does the Centre Vinicole de la Champagne.

A major challenge

Henri Macquart is now no longer responsible for drafting the president's report read out at the general assemblies. He was succeeded in June 1981 by his former vice-president Serge Rafflin[76], his right hand man from the early days. He had taken stock of the impressive achievements the Centre had made in its eleven year history when he sets new challenges with some of his colleagues. Excellent work had been done, but there was more to do. In his capacity as Honorary President, Henri Macquart attended all board meetings up until 1997, and saw the project develop over the years.

Things are looking rosy. Under his leadership, the Centre Vinicole de la Champagne has enlisted seventy cooperatives, providing them with a world-class, modern and highly efficient facility. Not only are production levels elevated (8,800,000 bottles produced in 1980), its members' coverage of the region and its several appellations is considerable.

75. François Mitterrand had been given a gift of bottles of champagne called *La Rose au poing*. The bottles were stored in the cellars before being auctioned by his widow.
76. Serge Rafflin (1923 - 2003), had originally come from the cooperative at Ludes. He was the Centre's first treasurer, and was president of the Fédération des coopératives vinicoles de Champagne between 1978 - 1983 and 1995 - 1999.

With this diversity of supplies, the CVC can set its goals high, aiming at a level of consistently exceptional quality. The investments made for pressing equipment and vinification machinery testify to the commitment shown by every member. We shall see the decisive role played by the cellar master in this respect later in the book[77]. Yet the cooperation's philosophy was always upheld, and its principles respected, particularly the three fundamental objectives.

The Centre provides its producers with storage space for 120,000 hectolitres, which was considered enormous at the time. With a dynamic president at the helm, the CVC supports champagne making and, in order to achieve its aims, it provides its members with a high performing facility. Last, and by no means least, was its continued successful sales strategy allowing semi-finished bottles to be sold specifically to the buyers.

The soloist of Chouilly is called to take centre stage at this orchestral concert played out by the members of the profession, the winegrowers and buyers and individual or re-grouped cooperatives. This, of course, is nothing more than a figure of speech, but it is a reflection of the inexorable changes dawning on the horizon. Since the 1960's the members of this "orchestre champenois" have been party to a redistribution of roles. Yet within the three sections of the orchestra, buyers, independent producers and cooperatives, there is not one who has not played a proactive part. Whilst investing in wine buying, and guaranteeing full brand visibility and autonomy, there are many French and foreign financiers who covet the "vin blond" so treasured by Apollinaire[78]. As they partake in a sip of this fizzing, festive libation, they discern a bouquet of success. Faced with larger agglomerations and regroupments, the independent producers invest and attempt to develop a sales strategy geared towards showcasing their own artisan products, yet by definition weak and isolated[79], they fail to impinge upon the balance of power. The cooperatives, on the other hand, increase their share of the market year by year. The emergence of regional cooperatives and unions, of which the Centre Vinicole de la Champagne is a key player, is a reflection of a desire to restructure the industry, and this is what motivates the cooperative movement. The fruits of this latest initiative taken by this group of pioneering individuals are nothing short of remarkable.

In twenty-five years, the buyers' business had grown by 33%, and the winegrowers'[80] business had leapt by 125%, who, what's more, they have sold eight times more champagne whilst the traders have increased their sales fourfold over the same period of time. So, both the independent producer and those belonging to a cooperative had gained far greater autonomy over traders. By the beginning of the 1980's their sales accounted for half the French market. Subsidies for construction and installation work mentioned before had a positive effect on the cooperative movement.

These subsidies could potentially cover up to 80% of the costs, and the loans given by Crédit Agricole made up the extra 20%.

With the onset of the 1980's things were looking up, with excellent harvests surpassing all expectations. The yields vary considerably, from between 4,353 kg/ha in 1981 to 15,012 kg/ha in 1983. The decade boasted eight quality years, four of which were memorable (1982, 1985, 1988 and 1989), and only two mediocre (1984 and 1986). This was a run of harvests of extraordinary success.

By the time Henri Macquart had handed over the Chouilly reins to Serge Rafflin, virtually everything the

---

77. See chapter "The linchpin: the cellar master".
78. "La nuit est blonde ô vin blond!" wrote the poet in his *Callibrammes* in 1918. But this is not the first time the adjective "blond" has been used to describe this nectar. The chronicler Thimothée Trimm (1815 - 1875) is known to have used this term in the columns of the *Petit Journal*: "Blond in glasses like a fiery topaz …."
79. The Fédération régionale des vignerons indépendants de Champagne was set up in 1992 and at the time had 22 members. In 2008 its membership base grew to 250. It is now one of the ten federations that grouped together to form the former Confédération nationale des caves particulières (the CNCP) which was later renamed the Vignerons indépendants de France (VIF).
80. This growth was stimulated by social policies regarding the granting of permissions for larger plantations, regulating land tax and ensuring efficient country planning. See François Bonal's book *Le Livre d'or de la Champagne*.

Serge Rafflin

Colleague and supporter right from the start of Henri Macquart, Serge Rafflin (1923-2003) originally came from the cooperative at Chigny-les-Roses. He was the Centre Vinicole's first treasurer and was later appointed vice-president was subsequently its president, a position he held from 1981 to 1993. He was president of the Fédération des coopératives vinicoles de la Champagne between 1978 and 1983 and 1985 and 1989. The praise is unanimous, Serge Rafflin "was a very dynamic figure who maintained cordial relations with all his directors". His son Denis remembers him as a "man of convictions. Much like one of Napoleon's cavalrymen, he went straight to the point". A pioneer "at a crucial time" Serge Rafflin is remembered as the man who took over from Henri Macquart and continued to develop the CVC, turning it into a state of the art facility. He supported the winegrowers cause and laid down the commercial foundations of the Centre.

Following in the founder president's footsteps, Serge Rafflin, originally from the cooperative at Ludes, was the first treasurer and subsequently vice-president of the Centre Vinicole de la Champagne which he then became president of until 1993. Here he is in the vineyards(1) and tasting the white wines (2) with his son Denis (on his right).

cooperative could have hoped for had been achieved. By the time the Centre had celebrated its tenth anniversary everyone's dreams had come true. The second president of a lineage totalling four to date was keen to tackle new projects some of which appeared almost revolutionary within a cooperative context.

What is important to remember is that the Syndicat and the Fédération des coopératives had "sincerely hoped for winegrowers to develop their work in champagne making[81]". In fact it was as far back as 1971, well before the CVC was set up, that Henri Macquart stated that "cooperation and champagne making are one and the same thing". All that the Cooperation needed was to develop its activities and that would clearly be of benefit to its members. It is unnecessary to cite an editorial of La Champagne viticole in which it was stated that "This champagne making on a small scale will lead to internal equilibrium within the industry as well as providing our members with a steady income that will take the winegrower out of his routine (sic), thereby fostering a sense of self confidence".

The issue of storage, quality, supply of services and sales that needed to be achieved by cooperatives was a major point of discussion. The figures speak for themselves. In 1968 less than 3,000,000 bottles were sold by a total of 24 cooperatives. Taking all the winegrowers into consideration, (both independent and cooperative members), this figure represents a mere 10% approximately of all consignments made by producers. This figure is more convincing when we take a global look at what was happening in the region, (independent producers, cooperative members and buyers). Champagne

---

81. Jean Nollevalle, quoted earlier.

cooperatives accounted for a mere 3% of total champagne consignments. The FVCV concluded that "There is an immense amount of work to be done".

Moreover, there is a balance of power in favour of the buyers, which has to be addressed at union meetings and dealt with. But in order to take decisive economical action, including regulating the market, producers must make themselves heard and sell more, much more. Many of the winegrowers are aware of the role cooperatives can play in altering the balance of power between vineyard and buyer. The SGV had tolerated, albeit with some reservation, the branding strategies adopted by some of the smaller cooperatives even though they were in direct competition with growers. Then when faced with a blatant desire to develop a branding strategy it had to concede to the fact that during the 1980's branded champagne found its niche more easily in sales circuits. Logically, this strategy fitted in with the producers' desire to be part of a competitive framework. It also improved the chances of striking a fairer balance between the principle players in the champagne industry within the framework of an inter-professional contract which was subject to regular revisions. In fact, it was at a general meeting held in 1982 that a marketing strategy was approved. They would remain true to cooperative ideals as the members, keen to see the strategy implemented, considered the initiative as a supplementary service.

The CVC is treading on new ground when considering its potentially large-scale marketing strategy. It is the subject of several board meetings spanning some considerable time; the idea of creating a brand is taking seed. Creating (or acquiring) a brand is all well and good, but bottles still need to be sold to consumers. Now, the vast off-trade distribution networks are an alien concept to cooperative members, and the labyrinth of international commerce even more so. Of course it is possible to get to grips with anything, but time is pressing ahead. And as the directors claim they know so little about it, why not try and find a business partner with a company culture and mission heavily involved in marketing? "Our approach thus far had been a little half-hearted, we'd not yet found a brand name, which did not help matters." The fact of the matter was, as stated by Jean-Pierre Daraut, that "without solid commercial funds" the CVC would not make it to the supermarket aisle end displays. The quest to find a solid and dependable partner started in earnest. First to be approached were the buyers based in the Champagne region, then the search extended to those operating outside the region. The Berger group[82] seemed to meet all the criteria. Its operations were on a wide scale and its network largely covered by Sales Representatives.

The deal is struck in Chouilly in 1983. A limited company is formed and given the name Compagnie des vins de Champagne. Firmly rooted in Champagne and with a picture of Reims Cathedral emblazoned on the label, the champagne brand Veuve Paul Bür should easily make its mark on the market. The brand is approved at the general meeting held on 27th May 1983. They failed to take account of the fact that the portfolio of Berger's sales reps was at variance with the champagne model. "Berger mainly dealt with syrups and its famous pastis. It also sold a small range of sparkling wines, but it had never sold champagne", the chorus of witnesses to this historic marriage chimed. The king of wines sat ill at ease on its product range, and the sales reps were not keen to push it. The champagne was only marketed once the reps had showcased the range of products they knew best to their clients who then weren't expecting to hear anything about champagne. It was poor targeting. The results fell well below expectations. This chalk and cheese arrangement had no future, and divorce was the only option. The company was dissolved at the general meeting held on 23rd -

---

82. Founded in 1830, the Berger group specialised in aniseed flavoured aperitifs. Over the years, it had developed a dynamic communication strategy (most notably with the memorable slogan: "Midday .... Seven o'clock, it's time for Berger!"). In 1995 it was taken over by the Marie Brizard group.

May 1986. Future boards of directors of the CVC would never forget this strategic blunder.

In the meantime bottles were piling up in the cellars, all the more so because of the phenomenal harvests of 1982 and 1983 (which had an average yield of 14,054 kg/ha and 15,012 kg/ha respectively). Nearly 4,500,000 hectolitres of grapes are harvested. Economic upheaval in the Champagne region is inevitable. There is also a danger that champagne may be devalued because of universal low prices. And lack of movement in the cellar means that value of the vins sur lattes will spiral downwards.

As a preventative measure, the visionary director had called in 1981 for the tank hall to be extended, but his pleas to the board fell on deaf ears. Extra containers had to be hired at the beginning of the harvest so that space could be freed up for the arrival of new grape must into the cellars. History was repeating itself and the dreaded scenario of uncontrollable stock levels experienced in the early seventies was rearing its head. Construction work started on two new cellars (numbers 13 and 15) but in was only until 1984 that they became fully operational.

And it was in 1984 that a new avenue was opening up for the Centre Vinicole de la Champagne that could prove most fortuitous: an acquisition of a stake in a company set up with traders to complete the supplies for the Moët – Hennessy – Mercier group. It took two years before the agreement was

ratified and the Mercier corporation was inaugurated and for the ball to be set rolling.

"We will rely more and more on sophisticated machinery. We have to increase productivity in order to compete in the market opening up before our very eyes and adapt to ever changing forces in the economy". This statement made by president Rafflin was calmly accepted by the members present at the meeting held on 24th May 1984, who accept the challenges ahead with renewed confidence. There is nothing in the statements that conflicts with the fundamental principles of cooperation, namely storage, champagne making, operating an efficient technical facility to produce a superb quality product (and in this respect technology is a valuable asset), a strengthening in sales and a credible counter-power to traders. Equally relevant to these achievable goals is the fact that the members remuneration is highly satisfactory. Serge Rafflin, also president of the FCVC until 1983, remains at the helm of the CVC and very much the driving force behind the team at Chouilly.

The facilities belonging to cooperatives are modernised in a bid to "constantly improve quality". In line with union ideals, the champagne cooperatives in the 1980's invest annually an average of 1,000,000 francs[83] in a bid "make its members self sufficient and improve equipment". In order to avoid ambiguity of any sort "From now on these investments will be made in a bid to improve the quality of our pressing and winemaking equipment which can only be of benefit to AOC Champagne." The tone is set at the Centre Vinicole de la Champagne and everyone knows that "Technical progress within the cooperative framework is central to our activity. The CVC must be at the forefront of technical innovation in Champagne." Part of the commercial development strategy involves the construction of a new disgorging hall and labelling unit.

1984 was a disastrous year for everyone in the profession and once more the need for vins de résérve is highly justified. It is Jean-Pierre Vincent[84] who stated that "our stockpile of vins de réserve bottled in previous years has enabled us to make some very fine blends and some very decent bottles have been produced." This led to the speakers at the general meeting held in May of the following year to state that "The sheer quality and quantity of the CVC's output is widely recognized by our commercial partners who regard the Centre as a valuable collaborator."

---

83. The equivalent in 2010 is a little over 150,000 Euros.
84. Jean-Pierre Vincent, appointed as Cellar Master in 1979. See Chapter "The linchpin: the cellar master".

The CVC attracts a growing number of visitors hailing from all over the world to its cellars in 1985. The managers see it as proof of "a flourishing interest in our initiative and the result of the members' concerted effort to make it a success". Every member of staff is congratulated on their involvement and ability to adapt to new circumstances "with an open mind" and embracing what computer technology and state of the art equipment have to offer in the "technological revolutionary times we live in", which promote "healthy competition in the industry".

It is at this point in time that the CVC explores new export avenues for its labels. The secondary brands Desroches[85], Saint-Maurice and de Prayères are launched abroad, amounting to three to four million bottles. They were to disappear from the market in early 2000[86]. With its average yield of 7,000 kg/ha, the 1985 harvest raised producers' spirits and the Centre Vinicole de la Champagne has good cause to celebrate. The grape must arriving at Chouilly was favourably compared with the must of 1975 which "had at long last been an extraordinary year". The cellar master noted that "Judging from the promising fermentation perfumes emanating from the cellars and the finesse, elegance and length in the mouth, the 1985 champagnes will be quite simply outstanding."

The big brokers are not always keen to buy wines from cooperatives, but the man Bernard de Nonencourt[87] affectionately calls the "Emir of Chouilly" holds courteous discussions with the cooperative which involve the participation of certain traders. "At Moët I frequently dealt with Yves Bénard[88], who happened to be an old school friend of mine from Montpellier." Louis Budin at Perrier-Jouët also held the work of the director general of the CVC in high esteem. There were further openings with the great champagne houses but it was a highly distinctive and unusual champagne producer with a vineyard of a few hectares nestling on the Montagne de Reims that changed Chouilly's fortunes for the better. A smooth, natural and compelling metamorphosis never experienced before in Champagne was taking place which would culminate in the Centre Vinicole de la Champagne occupying a uniquely privileged position in the cooperative movement.

All is revealed by the Centre's directors at the general meeting on 23 May 1986. What was to happen was to hail a new era in the industry. The issue of "stringent cooperation with the new marketing era" was discussed in addition to an equitable balance of power between producers and traders. This was reconfirmed by a prudent supplement stating "Everyone one of us has a duty to carefully review his position and monitor the performance of his own facilities", but, for the first time ever, the fact has been revealed officially for the first time.

A summary of the events of a year unlike any other is read out at the general meeting, which also provides an opportunity to congratulate independent wine growers who have recently joined the cooperative. However, the winter and end of April frosts have taken their toll on the harvest yields and the UPPCVC supplies account for just over 25%[89] of the grapes to be vinified. On the other hand, Aube was very seriously affected and its supplies fell from 14% to 5%. What is reassuring is that the production lines are back operating at full speed which translates into healthy profit margins. Yet what may not be picked up on in the president's speech, despite the fact that he made it official, is the announcement confirming the acquisition of the Nicolas Feuillatte brand.

---

85. This brand is sold still today in Great Britain at Marks & Spencers.
86. Today, the CV - CNF sells its own brand Veuve Émile at Auchan and at Great Britain's Asda.
87. Bernard de Nonencourt, born in 1920 was the president and director general of Laurent-Perrier (1949 - 1996), and has been president of the supervising council since 1999.
88. Yves Bénard, born in 1943, was the secretary general (1972 - 1979) and president of the board of directors (1979 - 1993) of Moët & Chandon, and has been president of the national committee for wines, cognacs and alcoholic beverages at the National Institute for traceability and quality (INAO) since 2007. He has been president of the International Organisation for vineyards and wine since 2009.
89. The supplies provided by the UPPCVC account for precisely 26% of total supplies.

The cooperative members believe that - for the time being – this acquisition made two months earlier equates to half a million bottles of which 40% are to be exported overseas. This represents a large slice of the market.

Be that as it may be, the acquisition of a brand by a cooperative is now in line with unionist policies, and this is unequivocally understood by its members when Marc Brugnon[90] makes his speech on the podium. "We are in a phase of full development", he stated succinctly. "It is absolutely essential we sell the product we make. We must be mindful of shoppers needs and be aware of current trends as we are in a consumer-led economy. Let us not forget that the French market could collapse because of weaker consumer spending. […] Europe's population is ageing and the Asian economy is the most dynamic in the world." So be it! It may well be, but the United States of America is for sure in 1986. As for being "up to date" the CVC has since its inception and increasingly so shown foresightedness. Many members of the board, the supervisors and Centre's members are well aware of, and do not doubt, Henri Macquart's entrepreneurial vision. It was Marc Brugnon who said "We must attach as much importance to our responsibilities as we do to the facility we have created", and is not sparing in giving out good marks to his members when he concluded: "When something happens at the Centre everybody in Champagne knows about it. This is also the case on a technical level as the Centre knows how to make Champagne of the finest quality."

But the eulogising was not over that morning at the general meeting as Jacques Houdard, Deputy Mayor of Épernay[91], speaking after the President of the SGV declared that "The CVC plays a crucial part in regulating the balance of power at a region-wide level". He congratulated the board members on their clear-sightedness and efficiency. This was praise that needed to be put into perspective with the idea raised on several occasions that day to train the managerial team.

90. Marc Brugnon, president of the Syndicat général des vignerons between 1978 and 1994.
91. Bernard Stasi was at the time joint mayor of Épernay.

1 - 2 - 3. There are two noteworthy numbers in 1986 that stick in the mind: 15, celebrating the fifteenth anniversary of the Centre and 100 celebrating the hundredth million bottle filled in March! This was a feat unheard of in Champagne.

In 1986 history was made with the first artificial heart implant[92], yet it remains to this day an unmemorable year for Champagne. The Centre Vinicole de la Champagne had reached a turning point by acquiring the Nicolas Feuillatte brand, and no-one to this day has fully gauged the consequences that have ensued.

The turning point

After the historic general meeting held in May, things were looking particularly rosy at Chouilly. Work in the laboratory proceeds apace and the effort put in by all the team yields very promising results. The finely-tuned analytical procedures involving the famous thermal shock to make wine achieved with state-of-the-art equipment and innovative procedures is a major breakthrough.

At the same time, research is carried out into the way wine develops after disgorgement and the taste of the cork. On the other hand, external commercial constraints dictate the need for fine-tuning the time-efficient systems used to analyse the way the wine develops and monitoring the mechanical processes. "It is with this in mind" states our narrator, "That the laboratory is fitted with pieces of equipment of even greater capacity, an automatic analysis chain and an atomic absorption spectrophotometre". This somewhat cumbersome term is the name for a piece of equipment that measures the level of metals (sodium, potassium, calcium and so on …) present in the grape must and wine.

There are two noteworthy numbers in 1986 that stick in the mind: 15, celebrating the fifteenth anniversary of the Centre and 100 celebrating the hundredth million bottle filled in March! 100,000,000 bottles produced at the CVC in fifteen years. This was a feat unheard of in Champagne. No other cooperative has beaten or indeed equalled this record. And in the history of champagne no "Maison de Négoce" can lay claim to having achieved this in such a short period of time. Two hundred years earlier just 300,000 bottles were produced in the whole

---

92. On 2nd May 1986 Dr Wilbert Keon and his team carried out the first artificial heart implant in Canada in order to keep an ill patient waiting for a transplant alive. The first heart transplant was carried out by professor Barnard some twenty years earlier, on 3rd December 1967.

region. This meteoric growth is unquestionably difficult to put into perspective when compared with the output of the other great and historic champagne houses. The size of the vineyard, the technical facilities, the disease prevention measures and the extensive knowledge of oenology are beyond comparison. The success attained was beyond everyone's dreams.

A succession of regulations decreed by inter-professional bodies, set out in a bid to consistently improve the quality of champagne, followed one after the other. Wine growers were now forbidden to add the liqueur de tirage before the 1st January following the 1985 harvest and were banned from using pressing machinery that dealt with loads lower than 2,000 kg.

It was during this decade that the trading faction of the champagne industry underwent major structural changes. There was a great swathe of acquisitions and mergers, and new groups began to proliferate. The family-run champagne houses began to disappear one by one. In 1984 de Venoge was bought by the Compagnie de Navigation Mixte and Pommery & Greno were now under the ownership of the Danone group (formerly BSN) who already owned Lanson. In 1985 two great brands changed hands: Joseph Henriot ceded ownership of Charles Heidsieck to the cognac giant Rémy Martin group and Henriot to Veuve Clicquot-Ponsardin. In the Autumn of that year Abelé was acquired by Spanish owned Freixenet, the world leader in sparkling wines.

Things move even faster in 1986. When Claude Taittinger, owner of the eponymous champagne house took over from Alaine de Vogüé[93] as president of the Syndicat of the great champagne houses after a public exchange offer, ownership of the Veuve Clicquot-Ponsardin (Henriot-Canard Duchêne) is acquired by Louis Vuitton. Moët-Hennessy follow suit and merge in September the following year.

Moët & Chandon, Mercier, Ruinart, Veuve Clicquot-Ponsardin and Henriot and Canard Duchêne merge with Hennessy cognac (followed shortly after by Hine), Père Magloire calvados, the haute couture house Christian Dior, the luxury suitcase makers Vuitton, and the Roc beauty products, and others followed suit. The repercussions of this seismic wave of extraordinary power were not just felt in Champagne. And one by one, the traders began relinquishing the grape pressing services they offered to wine growers and reverted to their original trading activities.

In 1988 work begins on the Channel Tunnel, and as far as all the merging activities go, the end of the tunnel is nowhere near in sight. In turn François Suez d'Aulan sells Piper Heidsieck to Rémy Martin, now owner of two of the three Heidsieck houses. The Frey group takes over Binet and Laurent-Perrier acquires Salon. The following year France celebrates the 200th anniversary of the Revolution. With the minimum fuss Laurent-Perrier buys Delamotte and Gosset Ivernel.

Buyers continue to gain ground quickly in the last half of the decade. Foreign conglomerates' appetite for the great champagne houses, clearly great sources of revenue and elitist jewels in the crown, was adding to the excitement. In the meantime, other houses wanting to avoid the risk of not developing and expanding in the appellation took control of other estates belonging to French and foreign wine growers.

There is clearly no comparison to be made between this horizontal integration[94] and the CVC's decision to buy the Nicolas Feuillatte champagne house. Yet clearly there were some avant-guard cooperative members who stop at nothing, so long as it was legally permissible, to balance the fluidity of the champagne market and first and foremost safeguard their independence from traders. Many harbour dreams of operating in a balanced market, though these aspirations are not publicly voiced.

---

93. Alaine de Vogüé had succeeded his father Bertrand de Vogüé in 1972.
94. The great family-owned champagne houses can be counted on the fingers of one hand.

Nicolas Feuillatte, his journey from coffee to champagne

Born on 29th January 1926, it was clear from the very start that Nicolas Feuillatte's future had already been mapped out. Born into a family of highly influential importers, he was called to succeed his father in running his portfolio of businesses which included Vernhes[95], the wine and spirits distributor supplying the cafés, hotels and restaurants of Paris. But it wasn't to be. He had several siblings, one sister and three brothers and he was not the oldest. Besides, Nicolas Feuillatte had an adventurous soul which motivated him to leave the cocoon of the family. Moreover, neither he or his father enjoyed a particularly close relationship. So, after the Second World War he thought he'd make a go of things across the Atlantic.

"Coffee was a growing market in the United States", recounts Nicolas Feuillatte. The Americans liked it and when I moved out there most of it was imported from Brazil. Africa, and in particular the Ivory Coast, produced, amongst other beans, high quality Robusta coffee[96]. A meeting I had with a diplomat from the Ivory Coast led me to importing it to the States."

It was hard going at the beginning, and then there was a taste of what was to come with a disruption in supply due to appalling weather conditions in Brazil.

The south east of the country had been hit by frost which destroyed plantations in the early 1950's. The big buyers came to us and sales of coffee from the Ivory Coast hit the roof. Instant coffee was at the time taking off and the earthier Robusta, not arabica, was the preferred choice for instant. This clearly was a boon for Nicolas Feuillatte. In 1960 he became the first importer of African coffee to the United States. His wizardry in commercial communication did the rest. As he explores potential sales markets he rubs shoulders with the "New York A-list" and hosts parties in his apartment overlooking Central Park. He plays golf with Aristotle Onassis and the Kennedys …

Nicolas Feuillatte savours every minute of his success and at forty is ready for new adventures. It was at that time, a new sign of destiny, that his brother Serge asked him if he wanted to join him in funding a project to acquire a 12 hectare vineyard in Bouleuse, a village in the vallée de Ardre, near Reims.

"I found the proposition both surprising and exciting", smiles the businessman, as speaking as a lover of great champagne and after a lifetime of giddy travelling around the world I asked myself what could be better than launching myself into this thoroughly French adventure."

Wine runs in the Feuillatte family blood. Wasn't Nicolas' maternal grandmother the biggest importer of Algerian wines to France?

The vineyard at Bouleuse, called Domaine de Saint-Nicholas, was restored and replanted. The first harvested grapes were sold to buyers. In 1976 the Feuillatte brothers decided to make the wine themselves and produce an elegant champagne with an original label displaying the signature of Nicolas Feuillatte. Jacques Girod, Director General of Maison Richard[97], recounts that in the early days Vernhes "had marketed a champagne under the Veuve Vernhes label" originally made with the grapes growing on the Bouleuse vineyard. The Nicolas Feuillatte brand was founded later and was "Widely distributed to the Paris restaurants through Spiritueux Vernhes".

Two years later they produced the cuvée "Réserve Particulière" mainly for Nicolas' American friends, most of whom belonged to the Gotham New York set. These celebrities, Jackie Onassis, Shirley MacLaine and Lauren Bacall, were regular visitors to Nicolas' New York apartment and his stunning Tunisian villa in Hammamet.

"It was then that I started taking an active role in the label's development not just in the United States, but also in France, Australia and eventually England[98]. It became an overnight success because of the quality of our wine."

It's fame was not just limited to the Champagne microcosm, but spread further afield as Yves Bénard's anecdote explains: "It was at the end of the 1970's that Frédéric Chandon de Briailles[99] asked me on his way back from New York "Do you know Nicolas Feuillatte? I met him at the Club 21 and he told me he was a winemaker in the vallée de Ardre?" I told him I didn't."

The champagne was selling very well, so much so that the Bouleuse vineyard was not large enough to deal with the increasing demand: Nicolas Feuillatte had to increase stocks with additional supplies from elsewhere.

"Most of the grapes came from the Union-Champagne D'Avize cooperative, but as demand for the product grew we had to cast our net wider."

---

95. Nicolas Feuillatte's father also imported rum, Vernhes had a total of 18,000 clients when it was bought by Maison Richard in 1985.
96. In the 1980's Brazil produced four times as much coffee than the Ivory Coast. By the beginning of 2000 it supplied twenty two times as much.
97. See Footnote 94
98. By the end of the 2000's Nicolas Feuillatte is the fourth biggest selling brand in the United Kingdom. It was Princess Diana's favourite champagne (according to Dominique Vrigneau, director of sales at Thierry's Wine Services, one of the biggest importers of French wine in Great Britain).
99. Frédéric Chandon de Briailles, born in 1927, was the former president-director general of Moët Hennessy (1976 – 1982). He also served on the board of directors (1971 – 1987) of Moët & Chandon champagne.

Nicolas Feuillatte is a formidable ambassador of the brand with crowned heads of Europe. Nicolas Feuillatte champagne had won over Princess Diana at an official dinner held at Windsor in 1991.

Nicolas Feuillatte loves welcoming his friends, many of whom are political high fliers and movie stars, into his New York apartment where he introduces them to the champagne bearing his name. Sofia Loren is one of his guests here in his villa at Hammamet.

The objective for the time being is to make the new acquisition as profitable as possible which, in more ways than one, differs quite radically from the other labels belonging to the cooperative.

It was absolutely not by chance that Champagne Nicolas Feuillatte was taken up by Chouilly. It all started with the extraordinary journey undertaken by a man who had had no previous links with the champagne industry.

Nicolas Feuillatte engaged the services of the outstanding champagne broker Rémi Paillard. It was whilst speaking to several cooperatives in a bid to find suppliers to meet increasing demands for champagne that he met Jean-Pierre Daraut at the Centre Vinicole de la Champagne.

"He asked me if I could produce some of Monsieur Feuillatte's champagne. I told him it was either to be all or nothing, because when the production of champagne is discharged to several winegrowers then lack of control and traceability become causes for concern. I would not have been able to differentiate between bottles produced by the Centre and those produced by other winegrowers. As part of a suppliers' network our reputation would have been damaged at worst or at the very least doubt would have been cast over the industry, had there been a problem."

Rémi Paillard reported what Jean-Pierre Daraut had said at their meeting to Nicolas Feuillatte who accepted the Director of the Centre Vinicole's terms and the deal was struck.

"The potential number of bottles involved was between four and five hundred thousand." The market proposed by Jean-Pierre Daraut and approved by Serge Rafflin and the board was a wise move on two accounts. Firstly it increased the CVC's production output and secondly because it added value to the brand's image. Nicolas Feuillatte champagne's biggest market is the US, with Australia soon to follow. Smaller quantities are sold elsewhere abroad and in France via Vernhes. Exports account for 40% of total production[100], a major coup for the CVC which as a result opens up new future markets. "I accompanied Monsieur Feuillatte on a trip to New York", recalls the former Director General, his champagne was on all the top restaurants' wine lists and distributed by all the big distributors …"

This is hardly surprising, as the Nicolas Feuillatte label is the tenth highest imported champagne in the U.S. In a bid to ensure the companies enduring success Nicolas Feuillatte cedes his own brand to the Centre Vinicole de la Champagne within weeks in a deal signed on 6th March. The Centre Vinicole de la Champagne now has full ownership of the label and all PR is now handled by the Centre, as contractually signed by Nicolas Feuillatte. From that date on, the Centre Vinicole de la Champagne has full ownership of the brand and is entirely responsible for producing the champagne as well as full control over image and marketing. Monsieur Nicolas Feuillatte continues in his role as the ambassador of the brand carrying his name. By proceeding in this way, the Centre Vinicole de la Champagne, made up of a group of cooperatives, does not sacrifice its soul. It's inviting its members to get involved in providing a supplementary service, but it is also taking full responsibility for marketing its wines, thereby guaranteeing an income to all those involved. It does not take long for the new venture to bear fruit. By the end of its second year 640,000 of the one million Nicolas Feuillatte champagne bottles produced are exported! Yet some cooperative members are quick to note that "The promotion of the Nicolas Feuillatte brand does not always result in good publicity for its secondary brands". Serge Rafflin counters by telling them that the CVC will act "like all big houses, [there are] some secondary brands waiting as many Nicolas Feuillatte bottles to be sold as possible". A clearer way forward could not be envisaged. Jean-Pierre Daraut labours the point by explaining that "when it comes to selling brands and products made in a large appellation, one is encouraged not to use the word "coop" particularly when it comes to exporting them as it may impact negatively upon our strategy[101]."

A happy compromise develops between winegrowers and traders. The negotiations held between Moët – Hennessy – Mercier which had lasted nearly two years led to the formation of Mercier SCCM, which became a client of the Centre. The CVC had a 35% stake in the newly formed company instituted in 1986, the year in which President Mitterrand appointed Jacques Chirac as Prime Minister.

By 1987, 90 people were employed at the Chouilly winery. Eager for expansion, the Centre's president Serge Rafflin began the hunt for a marketing expert.

"The incumbent was appointed Director of Commerce" Jean-Pierre Vincent recalls. Responsible for hiring staff and the new recruit's boss, Jean-Pierre Daraut laid claim to the title of Director General and promptly promoted every head of department of the Centre to Director. I was appointed Technical Director that very same day." The President was in agreement with the appointments. Jean-Pierre Daraut goes on to say "Initially, the Directors were reticent about investing in commerce. Then Rafflin took the horse by the reins. In my capacity as Director and Head of Personnel I eventually managed to recruit him. We were to go our separate ways later but the position was never again to be called into question."

The institution of a committee of Directors (director general, director of commerce, technical director and director of relations with the Champagne Region) was ratified at the general meeting held on 22 May 1987.

The statistics speak for themselves: in 1987, the Centre, made up of 69 cooperative members (about 4,500 winegrowers), saw a 20% increase in sales across the board. Exports were booming, with a 56% increase.

100. Up until 1986 the buyers were almost entirely responsible for the export market. The winegrowers and cooperatives were almost exclusively responsible for selling their products on the French market.
101. This conclusion was drawn at the general meeting held on 22nd May 1987. Today, this could not be further from the truth, as in Anglo Saxon countries, for example, a company with cooperative roots is of added value.

As part of a dynamic communication strategy embraced by personalities from the world of sports, here is an autographed photo of the champion cyclist Jacques Anquetil on a flying visit to the Centre Vinicole de la Champagne in 1987.

The Paris shop of the Centre Vinicole de la Champagne in rue du Faubourg-Saint-Honoré just moments away from the Champs-Élysées, was conceived as a shop and cellar, and is a sales platform for the champagnes made by the CVC. Today, renamed as the Espace Nicolas Feuillatte, it is a blatant reflection of the modern enterprise which is clearly embedded in the finest champagne traditions.

This significant slice of the market was cause for concern for some of those in charge who were wary of the volatility of foreign markets and who sought to encourage a more subtle balance between the French and export markets.

1988. The CVC produces 13,000,000 bottles (a proportion of which is given to the members) and the Nicolas Feuillatte brand (with 1,000,000 bottles sold) continues its upward trend. Those monitoring the markets find it hard to believe that just two years earlier "only" 400,000 bottles of Nicolas Feuillatte champagne had been sold. It was at this same time, 1,700,000 bottles were supplied to the SCCM.

The validity of their involvement with the SCCM was raised at the general meeting held in June 1989. The conclusion drawn was that it was handsomely paying off the loans incurred to purchase the equipment and in doing so they could maintain the cost of their services.

Yet all the while the technicians were trying to find new ways of improving production quality and efficiency, experimenting with clay paste[102], yeasts and alginate[103]. It was from then that the Centre used "selected bacteria" to induce malolactic fermentation[104]. This research testifies to the Centre's unflinching eagerness to look into how it could improve the quality of the wines made in Chouilly. The fruits of their perseverance, discernible in the wine's organoleptic qualities, translated into significantly increased sales. Sales of Nicolas Feuillatte champagne and its secondary brands leapt to 50% in

102. Clay paste can clarify wine as when a substance is added it can result in short or long term cloudiness in wine. In this specific instance bentonite, a clay that is an efficient absorbent and decolourant, is used.
103. Alginate is a salt of alginic acid used in the pharmaceutical, alimentary and textile industries.
104. Malolactic fermentation involves the transformation of malic acid into lactic acid which can lead to reduced acidity in grapes.

1989. Indeed, Nicolas Feuillatte sales tripled over a four-year period. More than 2,000,000 bottles produced at the Centre were sold that year, which represented a 34% increase over 1988. The ratio between France and abroad is clear: 60% of sales were destined for the French market whilst and 40% for overseas. The United Kingdom is the biggest importer of champagne with 500,000 secondary brand Desroches bottles sold.

These encouraging figures set the CVC minds at work. Why not supply airlines? Quarter bottles had to be made to meet the companies' stringent specifications. So, in 1990, the board of directors decided to invest in a bottling plant. And in the very same year sales circuits were developed in café-bars, hotels, restaurants, the prized CHR sector (Café-Hotellerie-Restauration) and off-trade distribution. In commercial terms all this is an important step towards much anticipated exposure, development and sales growth.

The joint stock company (Société Anonyme) Nicolas Feuillatte is set up in 1991. "The company's mission is to broaden the Centre's activities, with an emphasis on the fine wines, spirits and quality products associated with wine". Yet, by a series of events the company was not to fulfil its remit and eventually folded. The statute was reworked and the Centre Vinicole replaced the Société Anonyme.

An outlet in Paris showcasing the champagne was discussed (marketing at this stage in discussions was not on the agenda), reflecting commercial success. A shop was a viable option, a sales platform for the champagne made at the Centre Vinicole de la Champagne. By the end of the year this was to become a reality. Strategically yet discretely located within a stone's throw from the Champs-Élysées in an upmarket retail district, it epitomised the modern, forward looking company that clearly adhered to the best in champagne tradition. Nicolas Feuillatte takes pride of place on the display stands and subtly draws the attention of visitors to the shop, marketing itself as a successful brand. Following on from the success of Faubourg-Saint-Honoré is a second shop in Reims[105]. Other marketing initiatives ensue, including a partnership deal with Reims' major exhibition arena and plans to open an outlet at Eurodisney.

In November 1991 a retail outlet opens in New York in a bid to "gain full control of pricing structure and company strategy", and Nicolas Feuillatte is represented by an agent based near Southampton on the English South Coast.

Exports are going well in the Swiss, Australian, German, Italian, Spanish, Portuguese, Danish, Belgian and African[106] markets and sales rocket in Guadeloupe. This success is most welcome, particularly in these difficult times when the sky suddenly clouds over in Champagne.

---

105. The shop in Reims subsequently closed down. Another shop planned for Toulouse is an ongoing project.
106. The man behind the claims notes with regret that it is only the African elite that can enjoy champagne.

In the early 1990's, the Centre's total sales overreached the 2,000,000 mark. Sales of the Nicolas Feuillatte brand have tripled since 1986, the date the Centre acquired the brand.

The grand opening of the tank hall in 2005. It is only when the visitor is confronted with the imposing stainless steel tanks that he fully comprehends the sheer size of the Centre.

Once again a global financial crisis hits the world in the final decade of the century. There is a widespread drop in purchasing power which affects the Champagne region. The cost of grapes falls drastically, which has a knock-on effect on the region's winegrowers.

The roots of the trunk have taken hold; the branches and ensuing flowering should logically follow. But a new global crisis chills the euphoria of the 1980's, putting in jeopardy the balance that had been achieved. The cooperative movement cannot escape from the winds of reform blowing across the whole of the profession.

The ramifications continue

A new crisis rocking the financial world in its final decade of the century follow on from the petrol crises of 1974 and 1981. It takes root in Japan which finds itself in recession in 1990, and a decrease in consumer power spreads to the Champagne Region[107]. The price of grapes falls dramatically. The 32 francs a kilo in 1991 tumble to 24 francs in 1992, and shrink by a further 3,50 francs (20,50 francs a kilo) in 1993[108]. It was back in 1983-1984 that prices were at an all time low. The repercussions of the crisis are felt throughout the profession and leaders are faced with some hard choices. Some act on impulse and immediately reduce the cost of bottles. Others don't. "The directors of the CVC did not want to lower the price of champagne", a disgruntled Jean-Pierre Daraut recounts. "And it was because of their recalcitrance that we lost at least 500,000 bottles." Not everyone is in agreement with Daraut. Jacky Broggini[109], a Centre director, claimed that "Sales will not be boosted by lower prices" and Alain Robert, the third president of the CVC defends the policy decision taken at the time "We've never felt it necessary to lower the cost of champagne, not even in a crisis. It would only be a temporary measure that consumers would remember much later." "A pyrrhic victory" is still relevant today. The winegrower still enjoying the effects of the buoyant market of the 1980's during which record sales had been recorded in celebration of the two hundredth

---

107. The effects of the second Gulf war (The war of Kuwait) must also be taken into consideration.
108. This refers to the cost of grapes grown on a single grand cru vineyard. The average price of grapes is lower in the vast majority of cases, and was 6.54, 4.79 and 4 euros respectively in 2010.
109. Jacky Broggini, president of the wine cooperative at Chigny-les-Roses, speaking at the 1991 general meeting.

anniversary of the Revolution, was only later to become aware of this economic upheaval[110]. The ensuing repercussions would be more sorely felt and all the more so because at the time the cost of grapes was high, as was the cost of champagne. The consumer, the final link in the sales chain, was not buying champagne. Moreover, the hitherto respected inter-professional contract drawn up in 1959 was not renewed in 1990, and this resulted in a more liberal yet momentarily impotent market.

An official document[111] states that "The traders and cooperative movement were in full blown crisis in 1991. Sales slumped to an all time low, as did prices. It was impossible to justify the cost of grapes in this difficult economic scenario and the winegrowers' stocks kept piling up … we were all very gloomy about the prospects …"

Mindful of the difficulties, "and in a bid to prevent the brand carrying his name from losing any more money, Monsieur Nicolas Feuillatte, who was on extremely friendly terms with the president at the time, Serge Rafflin, renounced all royalties he would have received with each bottle of Nicolas Feuillatte champagne[112]".

Acutely aware of the crisis, the CVC was to play its cards well. The president announced at the general meeting on 29th May 1992 that since 1990 the brand's sales had increased by 7% and the Centre netted a 78% share of brand sales. Yet this percentage should be viewed in the light of total sales which had at the beginning of the 1990's fallen well below the 2,000,000 mark achieved in 1989. On the other hand, the number of bottles produced leapt by 2,500,000 between 1990 and 1991, and a target of 16,921,608 bottles was achieved whereas the bottles given to the members remained consistently at the 7,000,000 mark[113]. Serge Rafflin made no bones about the situation, concluding that "Each and everyone of us will have to make a concerted effort to come out of this particularly difficult crisis. The buoyancy of the last few years is a thing of the past, the market is in the doldrums and consumers are not buying champagne". The situation had to be faced up to and taking one step at a time, after having been invited to the 1991 VINEXPO, Nicolas Feuillatte champagne took part in SIAL 1992 and a handful of exhibitions overseas. In keeping true to the spirit of the founders, the emphasis rests firmly on achieving its original remit. In other words, no stone must be left unturned in the quest for maintaining credibility in terms of output and ensuring that the quality of champagne sets the Centre apart in the Champagne region.

Nicolas Feuillatte engages in friendly banter with president Serge Rafflin. Relations between the two men, and Rafflin's successor, Alain Robert were cordial and marked by feelings of mutual respect.

110. The industry is still facing tough economic times. The winegrowers feel the effects only after the retailers, wholesalers, négociants and buyers have placed their products on the sales circuits.
111. The history of the cooperatives written by the Fédération des coopératives vinicoles de Champagne.
112. These are the words of Sylvain Delaunois, president of the CV – CNF (in conversation with the author on 2nd June 2010).
113. This represents a little more than 24% of the total number of bottles filled in 1991. In 1973 70% of the bottles were given to the members.

So, confident of its state of the art facility and leverage in terms of capacity to compete in the market, the CVC with all guns blazing rises to the occasion. Quality control mechanisms are introduced in 1992[114] in a bid to monitor all production equipment, raw materials, processes and the finished product. The operation, aiming for "Quality Assurance" is called "zero margin for error". The CVC is one of the first organisations to implement this policy on such a wide scale. In doing so the CVC is in one way carrying out the Magister programme developed and instituted by the CIVC in 1991 whose objective was to apply phytosanitary measures, implement procedures when using products that minimise the risk of pest and plant infection and residues in its wines. Every effort is made to ensure that each member signs up to the policy.

1992 brings its fair share of regulations in strategic terms to the region. Pressing machinery must conform to set standards that must now operate at the same yield (between 150 kg/hl and 160 kg/hl), and a maximum of 4 hectolitres of rebêche[115] can be dispatched to the distillery and produced for personal consumption.

The slogan "Forget about contemplating your navel, take tough measures to set everyone back on track and let's get out of this mess" became very popular in the region the following year. Yet the Centre did not in 1993 adhere to those words by steering its suffering members onto the road of recovery. Just months later, stocks were piling up, sales of the new Nicolas Feuillatte brand were falling and business was far from rosy. The surface area of the vineyards owned by the CVC members had shrunk to the size it was in 1987. Consequently what the centre charged its winegrowers for services rendered to vinify their grapes was proportionally lower. This was not the first time there had been a dip in the surface area graph but an appreciable number of winegrowers had defected. "I knew all was not well". On the other hand the director of the regional headquarters of Crédit Agricole, Alain Robert was reluctant to admit that this could happen "In a field in which everyone could earn a living". He himself was a winegrower in Fossoy, a village in the vallée de la Marne and vice-president of the cooperative at Aulnois. To be frank, his winegrowing activities were just a small fraction of his successful career. His very first meeting with Jean-Pierre Daraut is firmly etched in his memory[116], and this is perhaps why he felt, more than anyone else, the air of tension reigning over the speaker's platform and the general uneasiness at the regional meeting he attended in 1992.

"It had all the atmosphere of a bazaar, the atmosphere wasn't too bad", recounts Alan Robert who having been fully briefed on the financial situation of the Centre took part in the meeting held in Épernay. He took to the stand to protest against how the situation was evolving. His speech entitled "All's not well, it's like working in a bazaar!" was received with icy coldness. Serge Rafflin and his vice-presidents arranged a meeting with him three months later and the gist of what was said was "Given you show great acumen, come and join the board."

As a man who does not shy away from challenge, Alain Robert accepted the offer. Once on the board he took part in a preparatory meeting for the 1993 general meeting. The latest recruit to the board felt his fellow directors were more concerned about the menu for the banquet than the balance sheet and what measures should be taken to sort things out. "It felt like no-one was in the slightest bit concerned about the fact that things were going from bad to worse in the shop. I just blew my top in the middle of the meeting …"

Serge Rafflin, shocked by this outburst, retaliated by saying "Robert, you are an astute man, get up from the table and take a seat over there" he said as he got up

---

114. The advertisement for the post of "Quality Control Executive" was made at the general meeting of 7th June 1991. Marianne Leclère is appointed. A "quality assurance charter" had already been implemented in September 1987. See Chapter "An avant-garde Facility".
115. Rebêche is wine made from the last pressings which is not used to make champagne.
116. They had met in the 1960's at a CIVC meeting. Alain Robert recalls Jean-Pierre Daraut, the young technical director of this inter-professional organisation bringing with him a plan for a union of cooperatives which he was to develop later in Chouilly.

from his chair "All you've managed to do is close the meeting!". Contrary to expectations Alain Robert took what the president said at face value, demanded a copy of the agenda and, leaving the directors to organise the menu, began raising questions of fundamental importance in front of the bewildered group.

Six months later Alain Robert became the third president of the Centre Vinicole de la Champagne, a position he held for seven years. This "coup d'État" had been achieved with Serge Rafflin's assent, whose tenure at Chouilly had lasted twelve years during which time he had presided over many meetings held in conjunction with the Fédération des coopératives vinicoles de Champagne[117]. According to some, Alain Robert's accession to the role, regardless of the volatility of his personality, was a logical step forward. The report of the ordinary general meeting[118] held on 7th June 1991 had registered Alain Robert's nomination to the post, proposing him as successor to Daniel Pétrus[119] in a bid to achieve a more balanced regional representation[120]. Serge Rafflin was the man behind the proposal as he was looking for a successor after having held the post for twelve years. "The role of president of a group of cooperatives is highly influential", says the man who was to give new direction to the Centre several years later. But for the time being he is successful man open to different ideas and who "is eager to take a new angle on things".

Alain Robert becomes president of the CVC on 4th June 1993. His appointment comes as something of a surprise to some of its members. For the first time in its history the Centre is not under the leadership of one of its founders. Furthermore, Alain Robert did not come from a union background[121] and had never sat in on any of the Fédération des coopératives vinicoles de Champagne meetings. He had for most of the time been an independent winegrower, a free spirit who had undoubtedly caused a stir with what he'd had to say at assemblies, but who had clear ideas that he wanted to implement.

The new president had within the organization a small margin for manoeuvre to pay off the debts incurred in purchasing the equipment and enlarging the facility and restore financial stability.

Some poor appointments had been made, this was particularly evident when it came to maintenance staff. Poor practices in certain areas led to lethargy particularly in the implementation of control mechanisms and clarity of documentation. Time saving strategies needed to be implemented to ease mobility between members and the Centre, etc. Moreover, highly valuable stocks needed to be shifted. And that translated into selling bottles.

But as seen before marketing was not at this time at the forefront of the Centre's agenda. "The board members sat at the table were more interested in their own cooperative than in the Union", claims Alain Robert. He was astonished by the fact that the cooperative members did not feel that the Nicolas Feuillatte brand (whose sales had, by the way, fallen yet again to 700,000 bottles) belonged to them. As far as the president was concerned there was only one option available to the Centre to restore equilibrium, and that was to introduce a commercial development strategy.

It was this that was to launch the Centre into being a pioneering organisation at the forefront of the Champagne industry. It was only later that the president du Syndicat des vignerons de la Champagne encouraged his members to follow the same path. In quoting Gaston Poittevin who said "The cooperation must be at

117. See footnote 75.
118. Resolution no. 4
119. Daniel Pétrus was president of the cooperative at Passy-sur-Marne in Aisne. He did not want to renew his tenure as president. The cooperative proposed the storage cooperative at the Vallée de la Marne in Aulnois as its replacement. As mentioned earlier in the book, Alain Robert was its vice-president.
120. This has always been the case. The board of directors tends to represent all its cooperatives and reflects in a balanced way the champagne appellation.
121. However, Alain Robert's father, André, had been the secretary of the Syndicat général des vignerons.

Alain Robert

"By sixteen years of age I was driving a tractor", fondly muses Alain Robert. Born in 1946, Robert is entirely self-taught. Unusually, he does not come from a unionist background and his interests are not simply confined to the world of champagne making. Nevertheless, much like his predecessors, he has always had the members' interests at heart, putting forward a range of services catering to their needs and ensuring they are well remunerated for their work. Overcoming the economic challenges faced in the 1990's was the principle focus of attention during his tenure at the Centre Vinicole de la Champagne. Having a now fully operational facility at his disposal, he developed its commercial activity on a much grander scale and conquered the global markets with the Nicolas Feuillatte brand. He has endeavoured to lead the CVC into exploring an external development policy. Take overs and merging options were also pursued, but these fell through.

the service of winegrowers", Philippe Feneuil[122] stated in 1999 that "It was our predecessors who created our cooperative and we've turned it into a successful organisation. But should we be aiming further? The answer is without question, yes, as long as we do not loose sight of our roots. We can make our mark on the export and distribution markets, nay global distribution, something the individual winegrowers selling his bubbles would never have been able to achieve. We must have the determination to get there whilst acting in the best interests of our members. Given this premise, the Syndicat should wholeheartedly support this initiative. Can we, together, commit ourselves and perhaps more importantly raise the funds to achieve our goals? We have no other option open to us as market conditions are changing as we speak".

The priority for Alain Robert now is to appoint a man with commercial vision who can rise to the challenge. The winning duo at the top must consist of a manager and developer, but within the context of the Centre Vinicole making the right appointment seems a distant dream. He himself combined the roles of president and director general since the end of December 1993, the year in which Jean-Pierre Daraut left. And this did not happen without some soul-searching.

Alain Robert, who had known the director general for many years[123], explains "I made my decision with heavy heart. Jean-Pierre Daraut had sacrificed everything for the Centre. He worked tirelessly, with heart and soul, and the profession owes so much to him."

Jean-Pierre Daraut remembers well the events of 17th December 1993 when the president and his board asked him "to take up retirement". The message was to the point, and there was no turning back. Daraut was to retire on grounds of poor health[124]. A realist, he knows full well that as early as when Serge Rafflin was president "he made some unpopular decisions that ruffled many of the board members' feathers[125]". Whatever the circumstances, one has to take responsibility for ones actions yet one cannot deny the fact that he had been an immensely popular director general "I announced the retirement of Jean-Pierre Daraut at an impromptu general meeting", recounts Alain Robert "there wasn't a dry eye in the hall. I found everyone's reaction devastating."

Still today everyone working under his leadership is unanimous in their praise of the man at the helm. "We were all affected by his departure", says André Patis. And this sentiment is echoed by another of the Centre's pioneer, Guy Lété[126]. Jean-Pierre Vincent says "Jean-Pierre breathed champagne. He was the guiding light of my work." Former vice-president of the Centre Jean Deliège puts him on a par with Henri Macquart. "President Macquart was an ideas man, as was Jean-Pierre Daraut. They made a great team."

In 1994 Alain Robert did what he could to recreate this outstanding partnership. He turned to the Head Hunters MF & Partners[127], and in no time at all several suitable candidates were put forward.

"It was both reassuring and rather amusing. Reassuring because we realised that the Centre Vinicole was engendering much interest, and it was an organisation that was being taken seriously. And amusing because there were some champagne industry heavyweights amongst the candidates." Michel Foutrier advised the board to cast their recruitment net wider in order to attract candidates from other industries. "I put forward an eclectic choice" he recalls. "And amongst the candidates I'd selected was Jean-Marc Pottiez who had not been involved in champagne previously and came

---

122. Philippe Feneuil, president of the SGVC between 1994 and 2004, speaking at the general meeting of the Fédération des coopératives de la Champagne which was celebrating its 60th anniversary.
123. See footnote 116.
124. Jean-Pierre Daraut suffered from sleep apnea, a condition that resulted in drowsiness during the day. "It was all so unfair", claims Jean-Pierre Vincent, "as he had taken the necessary steps to cure himself."
125. The Centre Vinicole owes much of its success to the president/director general partnership, a synergy of perfectly balanced power and mutual respect for the role and tasks each man had to perform.
126. Guy Lété was born in 1930. He came from the cooperative at Venteuil. As a board member at the Centre of thirty years standing he has known four presidents.
127. MF & Partners, recruitment specialists at supervisor and executive level, was founded by Michel Foutrier in 1981.

When Jean-Pierre Daraut, seen here in conversation with Nicolas Feuillatte, left the Centre in 1993 after having spent more than twenty years at Chouilly, he can be fully satisfied with the work he has accomplished. The facility he set up is one of the most modern and high performing to be found in the Champagne region.

from an interesting background." Jean-Marc Pottiez had not been a player in the champagne arena yet he had a solid background in wine markets[128]. However, contrary to the president's wishes who saw in him "a man who could get a grip on the situation", the board preferred a more conservative appointment. "I met with some fierce opposition", confides Alain Robert. "First and foremost from the board, then all the profession and those not connected with the Centre." The president still today has no regrets about having made his appointment. "His commitment to work showed no bounds and he is a remarkable developer." A frequenter of rally races since his youth, Alain Robert compares him to a formula 1 pilot, "The day you loosen the brakes, the game's over."

After twenty one years at Chouilly Jean-Pierre Daraut had good reason to be satisfied the day he left with what he'd achieved at the Centre. The winery was one of the most modern and efficient in the Champagne region. The Centre had grown naturally and gradually in harmony with the demands of its members and the market. Not only did it in every aspect meet the demands of continuously evolving vinification techniques, it also, in anticipation of consumers' higher expectations kept abreast of the latest technical developments by regularly installing state-of-the-art equipment[129]. "Jean-Pierre Daraut's plan had been carried out to its successful conclusion, and continued to be followed through after his departure", states his successor Jean-Marc Pottiez. "It is because of its solid foundations that the Centre is what it is today", underlines Jean-Pierre Vincent who was a close ally of the pioneering director for nearly twenty years. It was the sheer personality and ability of the man many of us called "Papa" that gave the Centre its momentum. He was able to guide the Centre because of his training and background in engineering and oenology in the right direction, allowing it to flourish and develop with strength and vitality[130]."

128. Jean-Marc Pottiez had been a key player in the revival of the Languedoc wine trade in his executive role at Vins Skalli – Fortant de France. See Chapter "The Conquest of a Global Market".
129. See chapter "An avant-garde Facility".
130. In conversation with the author on 22nd February 2010.

The foundations are well and truly watertight when Pottiez in early 1994 presents the facts as they are: the Centre has a membership of 85 cooperatives[131], amounting to some 4,000 winegrowers spread over 1,600 hectares. They have between them a total of 150 crus. 1,900,000 bottles were sold in 1993, a 12% increase on the 1,700,000 sold the preceding year, when the Centre faced a difficult time. Nearly 400 hectares of vineyards were used in the production of champagne designated to the trade, which would have been inconceivable twenty years earlier. The Centre employed 147 members of staff, including sales reps working for several brands, a far cry for the seven employees on the books in the early days of 1972. The turnover in 1993 is 500,000,000 francs[132], up by 20% on the previous year, for an initial outlay (and reserve fund) of 180,000,000 francs. The debt reduces appreciably to 250,000,000 francs (a 33% drop) as opposed to the 350,000,000 francs it owed in 1992. But there's plenty of stock in the cellars and prospects are promising. Somewhere between 11 and 12,000,000 bottles will be bottled "en tirage" and 7,000,000 will be riddled and disgorged. "With orders coming in thick and fast up to June 1994, this is a period marked by steady growth", states the former director general.

Faced with this half full or half empty bottle state of affairs as far as his successors go[133], the new team is determined to raise its game with the Nicolas Feuillatte brand and implement a more rigorous internal management system. Their objective is to reduce their stocks and costs. Clearly great strides ahead were taken in the 1980's (particularly in terms of the cooperatives' brands, partnership efforts, the acquisition of the Nicolas Feuillatte brand) but generated sales, buoyant though they may be, were not high enough and the average price of bottles too low to justify the costs in running the Centre Vinicole de la Champagne's magnificent yet colossal site. When it started at the beginning of the 1990's, the CVC was not the only cooperative with commercial ambitions.

Little by little the cooperative movement was taking hold and in the current difficult climate faced by the profession, the recently mentioned secondary effect was a priority. A credible policy geared towards commercial development was implemented in 1993. Pascal Férat[134], the president of the Fédération des coopératives vinicoles de Champagne recalled several years later that "In 1993 the FCVC began to focus all its attention on the commercial development of cooperatives". Its members stated that "We want winegrowers to be selling a 30% share of the champagne market[135]". And in this respect, the CV-Champagne Nicolas Feuillatte rose admirably once more to the challenge.

Jean-Marc Pottiez was recruited by Alain Robert as successor to Jean-Pierre Daraut. The two men were to form a successful working relationship that lasted from 1994 to 2001.

131. Counted in this are individual cooperatives that for the purposes of this statistic have not been re-grouped, as well as the 800 members of the Union of producers belonging to the CV.
132. 97,800,000 euros in 2010.
133. The new director general questions the entries in the commissions book of April 1994 which according to him only shows "the figures on finished bottles sold by buyers".
134. Pascal Férat, director of the cooperative of la Goutte d'Or in Vertus, was elected as president of the Syndicat général des vignerons in 2010.
135. The history of the cooperatives written by the Fédération des coopératives vinicoles de Champagne.

In 1994, the Centre Vinicole has storage capacity for 40,000,000 bottles.

This sumptuous picnic basket is indicative of the way champagne Nicolas Feuillatte has evolved, much supported by a marketing policy geared towards luring greater numbers of both French and foreign consumers.

PART TWO:
MODERN TIMES

The Centre Vinicole de la Champagne moves from strength to strength, its journey culminating in conquering the global market. Its ambitious commercial development and marketing strategy lures greater numbers of both French and foreign consumers. In creating a modern and bold image, Nicolas Feuillatte takes the industry by surprise with its innovative message reaching the highest echelons attained by the superb historical houses of Champagne. Yet the Champagne region faces some pretty tough decisions with the dawn of the new millennium. Anxious to plan for a peaceful future, the directors of the CV – CNF recourse to the fundamental precepts of the cooperative movement in a decade that opens up many paradoxes.

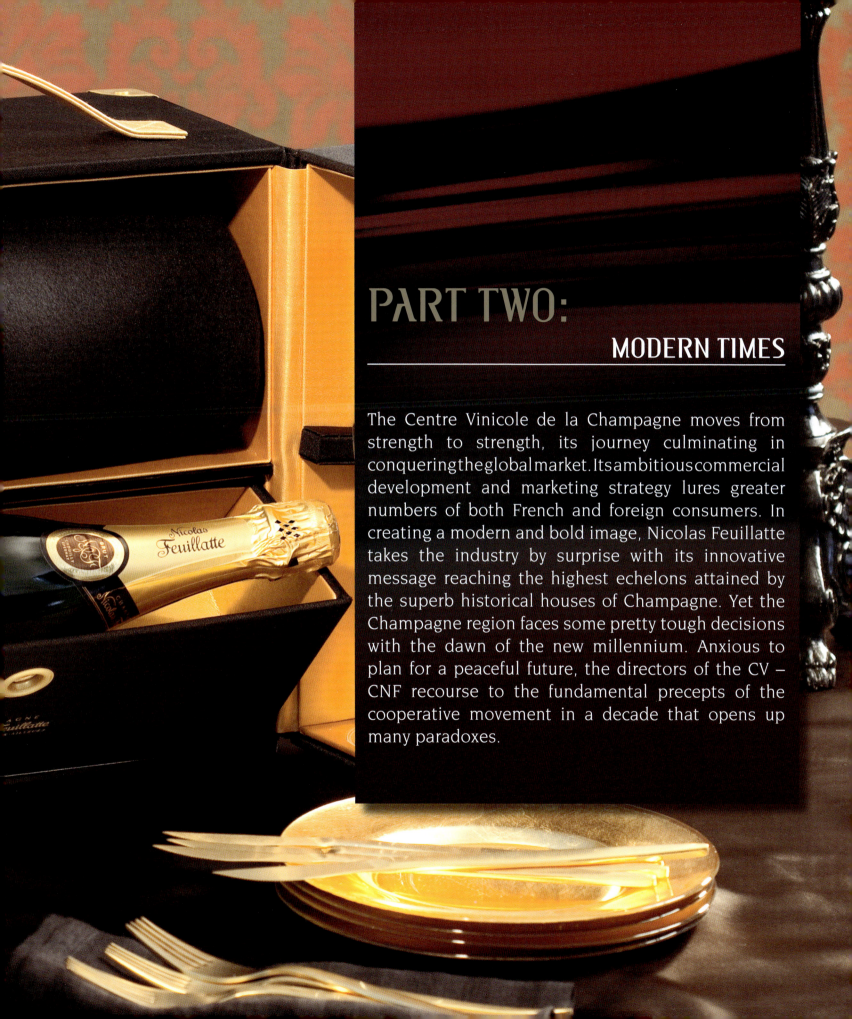

PAGE 88 | Nicolas Feuillatte, the champagne of the 21st Century

The strapline "Epernay – New York – Ailleurs" is emblazoned across 400 cabs whistling along the streets of London and Manchester during the ad campaign that lasted for the last eight weeks of 2007.

The Conquest of a Global Market

Financial crises, the anti alcohol protests (the Loi Évin[136] comes into force), a resurgence of popularity with the young in the traditional drinks market, increased global consumption of sparkling wines: obstacles are mounting. With its back to the wall, the profession reacts and the Centre Vinicole looks ahead.

Upon his arrival at Chouilly, Alain Robert decides on the course of action to be taken. He is quick to recognise that he must "immerse himself in the economics of the situation, as opposed to the unionist side of the business", departing from the principle that "Our strength lies in the economy, not the unionist movement which takes its impetus from the economy[137]". Yet despite his breaking out of his predecessors' mould the new president "is true to his cooperative roots". Top of his agenda is guaranteeing a long-term income for his members and their autonomy when it comes to selling their wine. He is also keen to establish balanced relations between cooperatives and traders, a recurring theme in the champagne industry. In his opinion, the winegrowers behind, or in tandem, with the cooperative should be able to work independently. "This is the reason why I came here. I wanted to get to grips with as much of the distribution chain as I could."

The target for the present time, in 1994, is to reduce the debt, and consequently the stocks, by implementing a robust commercial policy. By the same token "Sourcing had to be developed". Clearly he had to gain his members' implicit trust. The mission to reduce debts is top of the agenda and the new director general is granted full authority to act as he sees fit by his board. The second target follows on naturally aided by rigorous management and greater involvement from his members.

---

136. The Loi Évin of 10th January 1991 places stringent restrictions on how alcoholic beverages can be marketed in a bid to protect France's youth from an onslaught of marketing campaigns.
137. Interview with the author on 24th February 2010.

In April Jean-Marc Pottiez sets out some pretty succinct plans to reduce debts and stocks as much as possible and, most importantly, achieve long-term commercial development, which had recently been implemented. On a technical level the Centre was equipped with a stainless steel tank hall (with a capacity of 168,000 hectolitres), two tirage bottling lines (filling 13,000 and 8,000 bottles respectively per hour), 420 gyropalettes that could riddle 210,000 bottles a week), 2 disgorgement lines (disgorging 6,000 and 2,500 bottles respectively per week), two labelling lines (labelling 5,000 and 2,500 bottles per hour) and storage capacity for 40,000,000 bottles.

The first recommendations are implemented immediately. The new director general reassesses the pledges he made, renegotiates interest rates on bank loans, reshuffles staff, updates the catalogue, reorganises logistics, implements a staff rota over the summer vacation period, and so on. Again, in a bid to increase efficiency and make traceability as transparent as possible with relevant performance and management charts he invests considerably in computer technology, particularly in microcomputers, and information and communication technology. The enterprise is developing apace, switching effortlessly from an era of oral interaction to written communication.

The Centre is not undergoing a revolution, yet these adjustments are at times taxing to make. Mindful of this, Jean-Marie Pottiez focuses on commercial strategies and sales development in order to facilitate the movement of stock on a long-term basis. Achieving the second target is more complex. Strengthened by the course of events in the south of France mentioned earlier, the new director general throws himself wholeheartedly into the project. He takes a long, hard look at the client base and dryly proclaims that "Only four organisations in total have been responsible for sales: 130,000 bottles have been sold through the distributor Vernhes, 150,000 by Leclerc[138], 250,000 by Auchan and lastly Yvon Grimbard, the only agent operating in Toulouse has sold 50,000 bottles of

138. Marcel Verdes, Nicolas Feuillatte's off-trade representative in Brittany is the man behind the first commission (12,400 bottles) of the brand sold by the Centre Leclerc at Saint-Pol-de-Léon.

Nicolas Feuillatte Réserve Particulière champagne to companies and private customers, and 50,000 bottles of cuvée Saint-Nicholas, a second brand earmarked specifically for the corporate market."

The time is ripe for him to flex his muscles as an able developer. He appoints sales executives including Pierre Clamens who is in charge of exports, a key area to exploit. He also appoints capable agents, importers and sales representatives in Canada and Scandinavia. The commercial and marketing policy extends to the United States in a bid to boost sales of Nicolas Feuillatte champagne in America. The highly unusual and vivid blue label decorating the Réserve Particulière bottles is a bold choice, and one that much later on fits in with the brand's complete image. The dynamic approach is the same even though sales patterns and techniques vary according to country, be it the United Kingdom, Belgium, Scandinavia, Canada and Germany. Between the end of 1994 and the following year, the fruits of the new direction the Centre had taken were becoming evident, translating into a giant leap of 300,000 bottles sold of the Nicolas Feuillatte brand, and jumping from 700,000 bottles to 1,250,000 bottles in two years. The upward trend continues in 1996 with 1,800,000 bottles of Nicolas Feuillatte champagne sold in 1996.

It was during this period that the wholesale distribution sector was approached. The distributors Vernhes and France-Boissons are engaged to increase sales of Nicolas Feuillatte in restaurants, café-bars and hotels. This is how the champagne which had up until that point "filled champagne flutes at brasserie bars became a permanent feature in wine menus". Wine shops are also targeted to develop both the French and export markets. Within three years the brand has right

1 - 2 - 3. In 1994, the Centre Vinicole's armoury of equipment is enriched by a tank hall filled with stainless steel tanks (with a 168,000 hectolitre capacity), two tirage bottling lines (filling 13,000 and 8,000 bottles respectively per hour), 420 gyropalettes that could riddle 210,000 bottles a week), 2 disgorgement lines (disgorging 6,000 and 2,500 bottles respectively per week), two labelling lines (labelling 5,000 and 2,500 bottles per hour) and storage capacity for 40,000,000 bottles.

of place in all retailers' outlets. Eager to see the brand find its niche in the retail market, Jean-Marc Pottiez is concerned that Nicolas Feuillatte is retailed at a lower price than historic brands of comparable quality and renown and just behind the four or five market leaders. He and Président of the Syndicat général des vignerons de Champagne Marc Brugnon[139] are of the same opinion. "The aim of cooperation is to average out traders' prices", Brugnon declares in 1988.

This is achieved not without some wailing and gnashing of teeth. In shaking things up "with the président's consent", Jean-Marc Pottiez upsets many of his winegrowers and staff who accuse him of "messing around with the way things have been done at the CVC for years" and of "damaging the Centre's image[140]" by opting for wholesale distribution. The grumbles reach board level and in September 1994 a disconcerted board challenges Alain Robert. "The ground was disappearing from under my feet. They were out to undermine me." Things returned to normality when the president salvaged the situation by not hesitating to fire the vice president[141]. He managed to convince his fellow board members of the soundness of his ideas and let him pursue his policy. For the first time ever, a detailed account of sales of Nicolas Feuillatte was listed separately in the sales ledger of 1996. And with good reason because they verged on the 2,000,000 mark. Sales had leapt by 55% and the brand's value by 62%.

In the following year the Centre recorded "a 55% increase in sales of the Nicolas Feuillatte brand which hit the 3,000,000 sales mark[142]". But whereas in 1996 French sales grew by 54%, and exports by 58%, in 1997 sales abroad literally hit the roof with an increase of 145.8% in volume and 129.1% in value.

The work of the Robert-Pottiez duo was beginning to bear fruit. By this time the brand was solidly implanted in the market. Positioned in the top nine brands sold in the United States, Nicolas Feuillatte was also one of the top nine selling champagnes in the United Kingdom. Satisfaction was shared across all ranks. The Centre's members in particular applauded the "Nicolas Feuillatte contract" set up by Alain Robert which entitled them to a percentage of the sale cost of every bottle sold[143]. "It was a great idea, and proof of that is that it's still working successfully as we speak", says the former president of the Centre Vinicole. Again, as we saw earlier, Monsieur Nicolas Feuillatte renounced all royalties due to him on each bottle that was sold[144]. These policies led to the Centre making considerable savings throughout the 1990's given that the then current market accounted for the sales of millions of bottles. From a management point of view, this growth was most timely insofar as it enabled the centre to invest in new cellars, tanks[145], develop newproduction chains and renew necessary equipment when necessary.

---

139. Between 1978 and 1994.
140. There is a link between this and the stance taken by Philippe Feneuil who declared in 1999 that "[Cooperatives] should be in a position to make inroads into markets that champagne winegrowers could not achieve themselves, namely the export, distribution and let's admit it, the off-trade distribution markets." Quoted in the chapter "The Ramifications continue."
141. On the other hand, the president cannot fire the board members that represent their cooperatives as they have been elected by the members at the general meeting. They refuse to leave and remain on the board of directors.
142. More precisely, 2,935,000 bottles were sold adding to a total volume of all brands of 4,800,000 bottles. This was 1.8% of champagne exports and 22% of total sales made by the cooperative.
143. The Nicolas Feuillatte contract took up the inter-professional contractual remunerative system set up in 1959. This contract had not been renewed in 1989. However, set off against a longer term commitment (of six years' duration starting from 1996, and eight years starting from 2000, as opposed to the four years stipulated by the agreement signed with the buyers), and in a bid to adhere to the rules regulating good winemaking practices, the Nicolas Feuillatte contract delivered an added bonus to the winegrower who signed up to it if the average sales price of a NF bottle was more expensive than the multiplication coefficient of the average price of a kilo of grapes recorded in the appellation (source, the CIVC). It was an added bonus to the winegrower who followed good viticultural practises, and was based on the volume of supplies. The Nicolas Feuillatte contract was subject to regular modification and refinement. The last version dates from 2009. Today, the remuneration equates to 34% of the price of the bottle sold to the consumer.
144. These royalties were received after Nicolas Feuillatte had sold his brand to the CVC. See chapter "The Ramifications Continue".
145. The tank hall was enlarged by 2,400 square metres and 36 tanks with a 900 hectolitre capacity were installed. However, the project for two additionally planned cellars was aborted in 1998.

The Brut Réserve Particulière is served on board Poerava Air Tahiti Nui's first and business class flights. Nicolas Feuillatte had been selected by several airlines to be served on board since the early 1990's. In 2008 the magazine *Global Traveller* ranked Nicolas Feuillatte champagne as one of the best wines available on business class flights.

An unexpected avenue opening up new perspectives presented itself to the Centre Vinicole and its Nicolas Feuillatte brand. Jean-Marc Pottiez tells the story. "Jean-Pierre Daraut had purchased a machine[146] that could transfer the wine from 750ml bottles to quarter bottles, which is the most beautiful in the entire region and from a technical point of view the best insofar as it in no way impinges upon the quality of the wine. The idea was to have a piece of equipment that could be used by other cooperatives as well. This never happened and consequently the siphon was too large for the Centre's needs back in 1994." It was working to a 10% capacity as no-one else was using it, so the president tried to pass it on somewhere else. "Piper-Heidsieck was interested, but we never got round to selling it, and thank goodness!" recalls Jean-Pierre Vincent.

The Centre then looked into selling it on the booming airlines market[147] as they had a growing interest in buying not only full sized but more importantly quarter sized bottles[148]. In 1996 the directors accepted Servair's offer, the subsidiary of Air France.

The equipment had to meet the qualitative (the selection was made by a strict committee), quantitative (several hundreds of thousands of equivalent bottles for the international company) and technical standards (the quarter bottles were screw capped, which presented a new set of challenges).

146. This machine is still in use at the Centre Vinicole – Champagne Nicolas Feuillatte, and siphons the content of the bottles of champagne into another container of different dimensions, most notably the 20 centilitre quarter bottles. Equal amounts of pressure are found in the empty bottles, and the liquid that has been drawn by suction does not release its carbonic gasses.
147. The director general, when he was in the Languedoc, and Pierre Clamens, who was at the time director of exports at the Laiterie Coopérative d'Isigny-Sainte-Mère, had already approached this clientele. Their experience was of fundamental importance.
148. For logistical reasons, the vast majority of airline companies have today replaced their quarter bottles with traditional champagne bottles. This is much regretted by the suppliers who have noted a marked diminution of brand visibility on board.

By the same token, the kudos attached to providing a service to an international airline was unquestionable. From a marketing and communication point of view, the brand's presence in the airline industry is of immense value, worthy of the best marketing campaign. And lastly, the Centre's members many of whom travel by air can feel justifiably proud of **their** brand. It also presents the board with the opportunity to unite the staff working at the Centre "into a technical-commercial-PR-adminstrative success".

"Our initial foray into the airline business was not particularly fruitful", recounts Jean-Marc Pottiez, "but at least we'd made it into the market." Nicolas Feuillatte seize half the market of the French airline, with nearly 500,000 bottles sold in 1997. Feuillatte is drunk by passengers choosing to fly economy and business class. Vintage Feuillatte is served in first and business classes, and quarter bottles of Brut are served at every meal served in economy class on long haul fights. The cuvée Palmes d'Or is available on the prestigious supersonic Concorde flights. By this stage, Nicolas Feuillatte is competing with Charles Heidsieck, Piper-Heidsieck and Krug belonging to the Rémy-Cointreau group, with whom they share equal market share.

Quality and savoir-faire have paid off. "It is true that we'd been making quarter bottles for our trading partners for some time[149]. It was a well known fact", adds the former director general. What did not protect us from criticism, also targeting Air France who "were emerging from a delicately critical period at the time", he confirms. Reports in one American newspaper even said that the French company would stoop to selling champagnes made in a cooperative!" These blows below the belt did nothing to stop us from renewing the contract the following year. It worked out even better for us as orders doubled because many of the traders who had replied to the invitation to bid at the end of 1997 moaned about sharing the Centre Vinicole's supplies of champagne with Air France. According to Jean-Marc Pottiez "offers were made by certain trading partners on the condition that Servair would not come to an agreement with a cooperative". This was unpopular with the directors of Servair who guaranteed an exclusive contract in 1998 with the Centre Vinicole for the supply of 1,050,000 bottles of Nicolas Feuillatte. And it was the same for the following year.

"All of a sudden we were everywhere", he continues. In commercial terms, Nicolas Feuillatte was going from strength to strength with its firm foothold in the United States, presence at the Hilton hotel chain firstly in France, later expanding across Europe, thereby consolidating its meteoric development, due in large part to a commercial policy instituted by those with relevant expertise."

The impact is phenomenal on consumers and winegrowers who see their champagne brand on planes they take themselves. "The day the deal was struck between Nicolas Feuillatte and Air France, interest in Nicolas Feuillatte rocketed, and in a sense the brand became synonymous with the airline."

Alain Robert rejoices in the fact that "The Nicolas Feuillatte brand really took off and it is because of the team's efforts to pursue a new commercial policy that we today hold a 25% market share in champagnes made and marketed by a cooperative operating in Champagne". The Centre Vinicole is a model cooperative which all cooperatives should aspire to. It is a charismatic organization that continues to attract members, so much so that additional supplies rose by 12% in 1996. The Centre has a total of 1,900 hectares at its disposal, equating to 6% of the champagne appellation. All the same, its president encouraged his members to "work together in constructing a site of which they are the owners".

Between 1994 and 1996 Alain Robert and Jean-Marc Pottiez focus their attention on commercial development. It is essential that their radical distribution policy is supported by bold marketing

149. Perrier-Jouët, and others.

and targeted communication for it to succeed on a long-term basis. And this is what the director general working closely with his president knuckle down to between 1997-1998. "Our Air France coup opened up new and interesting horizons to explore[150]. But we had to move up a gear. Nicolas Feuillatte had to have its rightful place amongst the great and historic French labels." We needed to engage with the public and assess the situation:

- if it's not as widely known as it should be it is because the brand does not have ubiquitous presence.
- It has only been going for fifteen years and is part of a market where the centuries' old brands "have invented a heritage and past for themselves" - it's image is negatively affected by its cooperative origins, often referred to in the press as "a gigantic industrial facility", and an "enormous cooperative".

The president and his director general agree to make light of these setbacks and focus on the company's youth "We're fifteen years old and looking towards our future!". Aiming to compete more effectively in the market they take a gamble with their consumers image. "When looking at consumers' behaviour" says Jean-Marc Pottiez, "I see no desire for young champagne lovers to have the same tastes as their fathers. A consumer in his thirties or forties beginning to take a real interest in champagne is looking to discover other champagnes that are not drunk by his parents. This was really something to aim for." Alain Robert concurs, "It was Pottiez's idea to develop the brand's younger image." The message was clear: we were certainly not going to change the image of this exquisite nectar into a champagne without a clear identity, and it was far from our intention to reject the traditional image of the product.

At the end of the 1990's the Centre approached three communication agencies, providing them with a brief on what they hoped to achieve on a long-term basis. "We had no contact with them for ten whole years. Two of the three agencies failed to deliver, it was Callegari-Berville[151] that fully understood what we were after."

Jean-Marc Pottiez was well aware of the fact that the company was proud of its roots, despite not having a historic heritage. "Not a single brand back in 1998 was talking about the work carried out by winegrowers. A tour of a champagne house began with the blend, and that was that!" He recalls what Robert had to say on the subject, "Our brand is young, but let's not forget that our shareholding winegrowers have for generations known how to ripen grapes in what is one of the most difficult environments in France!" So, "to anchor this brand firmly into the terroir was a brilliant idea, so long as we did not play the beret and baguette card!". In other words we had to steer clear of a clichéd idealised image. This was a pivotal message conceived by a creative partnership that was soon to exploit the brand's image to the full.

The Nicolas Feuillatte brand had another challenge to overcome. It wanted to internationalise the brand within the context of this "new look" strategy, and its presence on Air France provided the perfect opportunity. Lastly, yet another challenge presented itself to the new image makers, and that was that it was impossible to market a bottle of Nicolas Feuillatte Brut as there were three presentation models on the market[152].

Spurred on by the new challenge, Callegari-Berville threw themselves wholeheartedly into the project, coming up with an original concept revolving around travel and universality and happiness that broke away from the drink's traditional image. Importantly the Centre Vinicole was entirely satisfied with the fees the agency charged them for the campaign[153].

---

150. Other international airlines followed suit, namely SAS, ANA, Air Lingus, Corsair, South African Airlines …
151. The communication and publicity agency set up in 1986 by Pierre Callegari and Pierre Berville. It was Pierre Berville who was mainly involved in the Nicolas Feuillatte campaign.
152. For off-trade, distribution, the CHR circuit and the U.S. Market.
153. The fee was approximately 1,000,000 euros.

CHAMPAGNE
Nicolas Feuillatte
EPERNAY - NEW YORK - AILLEURS

"The campaign was launched in March", an enthused Jean-Marc Pottiez recalls. "This was unusual as the majority of marketing campaigns are launched at the end of the year. We opted for more costly classic urban billboards and bus shelter campaigns". Our displays were featured on in excess of 16,000 bus shelters spread over 650 towns with more than 20,000 inhabitants. They were everywhere. The campaign really took off when "Callegari-Berville" came up with the strap line "Chouilly – New York – Ailleurs. All I wanted was to replace Chouilly with Épernay, a place of universal appeal[154]."

Keen to make the brand's identity relevant to current society, from the moment Jean-Marc Pottiez set foot in the Centre he harboured dreams of linking Nicolas Feuillatte champagne with contemporary art. He had in the past created a successful synergy between art and wine[155], and believed that Nicolas Feuillatte champagne could partner artistic achievements beautifully.

"I had several meetings with people who were involved in art at a regional level to discuss my idea of forming an association between an artist and the brand, but nothing came of it. I hoped that the man or woman we'd chosen would be someone who'd not only create a work of art that was inspired by our champagne, but also highlight the milestone's our enterprise had achieved over the year." Widely misunderstood, he went round and round in circles until he appointed a new director of marketing and communication, Andréa Buchin[156] in 1998.

> The champagne Nicolas Feuillatte stands out with its strap line l'ailleurs – or beyond – which conjures up images of getting away from it all in faraway destinations and through the passing of time.

"Everything suddenly became clear and within a month of her arrival we'd taken all the crucial steps in finding an artist in residence who would encapsulate in his work all the Centre's work over the year", says Jean-Marc Pottiez.

Marie-Claude Le Floc'h, the director of Courant d'Art, a company based in Paris advising on contemporary art, put forward a selection of artists[157]. They each had to produce a work based on a champagne related theme of our choice. The themes we proposed for the next three years were Terroir[158] (1999), Time (2000) and Space (2001). It was our intention that each original work be exhibited at the Centre and reproduced on our greeting cards, writing paper, press releases, brochures, promotional material, and so on. A limited edition of 1,000 luxury brochures was also printed on the same theme and presented to VIP celebrities, faithful clients and executives working in the profession[159].

---

154. See the later chapter "Boldness & Communication".
155. Around la Figuration Libre (Free Figuration) and the école de Sète.
156. Coming from Guy Degrenne and the Hermès group (Saint-Louis crystal and Puiforcat designer tableware), Andréa Buchin was the director of marketing at the Centre Vinicole between 1998 and 2001.
157. See chapter "Boldness & Communication".
158. Marie Thurman was the first in a long succession of artists-in-residence forming a year long association with Nicolas Feuillatte champagne. See the chapter "Boldness & Communication".
159. Only two brochures were produced (*Le Terroir* and *Le Temps*). The printing, thought to be too elitist and costly, was abandoned in 2001.

The project still runs today, the original spirit of the programme very much intact. It expanded further in 2002 with the institution of the Prix Nicolas Feuillatte for Contemporary Art with the prize money going to the artist in resident. Bruno Bressolin was the first recipient honoured with this prize which is handed out every year[160].

Today, the works exhibited in the Centre's buildings do not cause internally within the organization stirrings amongst the ranks, but the reaction was quite different in the early days. "Generally speaking even if the staff found the artists' style a little too adventurous they were still proud to have his works taking centre stage in their workplace."

Aware of the fact that the traditional brands decorated their bottles with standard labels for the U.S. market, the Centre set about decorating their Nicolas Feuillatte bottles with innovative packaging. Metal and PVC boxes illustrated by artists began appearing on the market. This youthful image was replicated on several champagne accessories, including sommeliers' aprons and a whole range of consumer objects.

Jean-Marc Pottiez was also keen to develop another area, and that was to forge a closer relationship between the winegrowers and technicians working at the Centre Vinicole. "I remember well being obsessed by the idea of integrating the winegrowers fully with the technical team working at the Centre. We had to formalise communication methods with the winegrowers as no formal means of communication had been previously instituted. Matters of communication with the winegrowers had always been dealt with by the CIVC."

A journal intended for internal circulation was created[161]. We took note of the arrival of technicians specialised in dealing with winegrowers in 1995. Later the PR team is augmented in order to "maintain effective dialogue between members and meet as best as possible their needs, showing flexibility, but also promoting the image to our visiting clients of the working winegrowers producing Nicolas Feuillatte."

The fact that Dominique Pierre, the Deputy General Manager, is responsible for carrying out this service translates into a highly effective move. Alain Robert had hoped that the man in direct contact with the winegrowers would be a close ally and as he knows the industry like the back of his hand, he is someone in whom the winegrowers would have complete confidence. The scope of the project included improving the means of communication amongst the winegrowers and offering support to traders by providing information on what was happening on the vineyards. Meetings were to be

In anglophone countries, here we are in New York's Manhattan, the strap line "Épernay, New York, Ailleurs" is translated into English, but phonetic guidance is given, *say it [foyat]* to assist in the pronunciation of the name Feuillatte.

160. See chapter "Boldness & Communication".
161. The journal is specifically aimed towards the winegrowers, a second journal, *Plumecoq*, is distributed amongst the employees.

attended by winegrowers who in their villages tried to change their ingrained habits, and even traditions. A sharing of knowledge would mean that the industry could develop even quicker.

"We were the innovators of the region who had instituted a rigorous policy of communication" says Jean-Marc Pottiez. Yet these changes were met, in the early days, with some opposition. Some members of the cooperative and board were happy with the system that had been in existence since the CVC had been set up and were generally speaking sceptical of reforms they believed meddled with the "structure and technical aspects of their work". They had to be reassured and convinced that these reforms were necessary. Old equipment was replaced with new, and money was invested into the Centre which the members themselves contributed towards. New tanks were bought and cellars built, testifying to the director's desire to move things forward, and this armoury of new technological equipment is proof of the confidence they have in the brand. Sophisticated equipment measuring the sugar content in grapes (colibris) contributed towards the self sufficiency of the winegrowers[162].

In 1999, Alain Robert updates his members on the parameters of the essential work that needs to be carried out which had been "clearly outlined to the Chief Executive Officer". In the first instance, and as a result of improved performance on the technical front of the CVC's operations Alain Robert claims "We can fully guarantee the quality of our wines. We have met certified standards, invested in ecologically sustainable equipment and promoted our work on improving the quality of the grapes and must we use in making our champagne."

Continued research into quality is something the Centre has always striven towards. Jean-Pierre Daraut had in his time fought for "zero margin for error". The application of a "quality charter" in 1987 and a "Quality Service Policy" in 1992 are further proof of everyone's commitment. A "Quality Assurance" strategy is widely discussed and the CVC is one of the first to implement it. Upon his arrival at the Centre Vinicole, Jean-Marc Pottiez continued to progress the work already achieved and implement the strategy outlined at the general meeting of 3rd June 1994 which would see the formal application of the ISO 9002 certification[163]. President Robert took advantage of the arrival of "investigators who analysed everything. The ISO certification enabled me to find out how everything worked at the Centre", he adds wryly. This was taken up by the Chief Executive Officer for whom "a quality assurance policy is a mean to understand fully what goes on in the Centre and to delegate further responsibility to every man working at every level of the hierarchy, including those at the bottom".

The certification is re-applied the following year and "makes the Centre Vinicole one of the 28 French pilot companies (and one of two companies operating in the agro-alimentary sector) chosen to test the new ISO 9001 certification implemented in 2000."

Previously in 1996, quality assurance was independently implemented in the Centre Vinicole and the post of director of quality assurance, food safety and the environment was created. Marianne Leclère[164] who was known for her rigorous approach in such matters, was welcomed with open arms by Jean-Marc Pottiez in 1998[165]. There was only one way to achieve the achievable, and that was done by talking and helping the winegrowers to develop sustainable winegrowing practices which involved the minimum use of chemicals. Meetings had to take place and information transmitted to the relevant parties. It was decided in 1996 that seminars should be held three times a year[166], a move that was

162. This equipment enabled the winegrowers to assess the maturity of their grapes without having recourse to external interventions.
163. The ISO 9002 certification complying with the Quality Assurance system was obtained in 1996 and reconfirmed in 1999.
165. Quality assurance has been subsequently dealt with by heads of department after the departure of Marianne Leclère in 2002, namely Muriel Faye and Christophe Landat who is today responsible for sustainable development (see chapter "An avant-garde facility").
166. In conjunction with the council for winegrowing in Montpellier.

In the early days, the works exhibited in the Centre's buildings caused within the organization stirrings amongst the ranks. If the staff found the artists' style a little too adventurous they were still proud to have his works taking centre stage in their workplace. Today, works of art are beautifully integrated in the Centre.

popular with all concerned. These seminars were attended "by the Centre's winegrowers who combined forces to achieve an ecologically sustainable integrated production of champagne which offered 21st century consumers a safe and quality product". The focus of attention over the year was the construction of a water treatment plant for which a considerable sum of money was invested. The plant was large enough to be capable of supplying a town with 27,000 inhabitants and cost the best part of the 23,000,000 francs[167] that had been allocated to quality improvement measures.

As was to be expected, research into a higher level of safety standards ensued rapidly, as well as the implementation of an eco-environmental policy. Nicolas Feuillatte champagne, one of the leading brands of its time, fell flat on his feet when it came to embracing long-term development. Successive boards were to continue and widen the scope of the company's commitment to the ecology[168].

Lastly, in the opinion of the former Chief Executive Officer "our pre-winegrowing marketing policy had played a crucial role in how the board of directors' communication strategy performed. It led to an external expansion which was imperative for winegrowers".

In 1998 euphoria had swept across the board, reaching out to even the most hard headed. An exalted Jean-Marc Pottiez took to the podium, addressing his members gathered at the general meeting on 23rd April 1999, "Were we to make a comparison with rugby, a sport held so dear by the Nicolas Feuillatte brand which sponsors many of the 1st division clubs[169], 1998 could be considered by the CVC as a "trial year", a crowning achievement of five years of hard work, during which the work carried out by an impeccable team has grown from strength to strength, and led to a firmer partnership between the member cooperatives and staff."

The statistics speak for themselves: the number of bottles produced is tenfold higher than in 1973[170], 8,400,400 bottles were sold at an average pre-tax price of 60 francs[171], of which 5,000,000 were

167. Approximately 3,500,000 euros.
168. See the chapter "An avant-garde facility".
169. Today, they are called the Top 14.
170. A new bottling and tirage line (working at a rate of 20,000 per hour) is installed.
171. A little more than 10 euros.

Nicolas Feuillatte, sold at an average pre-tax price of 68 francs. Everyone involved was of the same opinion as the president Robert who stated that "Le Centre Vinicole de la Champagne can face its future with serenity".

As 1999 draws to an end, the decade and century could not conclude on a higher note. "The 20th century has culminated in a high point", notes Jean-Pierre Vincent in his cellar journal. We've never seen a harvest like this before, it's been the least acidic and the most plentiful. The average yield was 12,989 kg/ha." The champagne produced by the Centre Vinicole was made with vineyards spread across 1,950 hectares, an increase of 300 hectares in five years. The board concluded that the measures it took wholly satisfied winegrowers' expectations. The plan was not even remotely connected with harvest issues, yet for Jean-Marc Pottiez it was nevertheless "a fantastic year. I had no other option open to me other than to ration our clients' supplies. We had to set the limit at six bottles when we had orders for nine. We even had to delay opening new markets in the world."

Alain Robert is measured when making observations on the targets the Centre has achieved, and he is cautious about a less radiant future, "I think it is essential we reaffirm our commitment to exploiting our agricultural roots which are a credible force in an industry managed by dwindling numbers of professionals from the region."

This analysis of the situation supports the fact that in order for a federal group to conquer the market, the winegrower himself must feel above all independent.

1999 finishes off the decade on a high note. The champagne produced by the Centre Vinicole in that year alone was made with vineyards spread across 1,950 hectares, an increase of 300 hectares in five years.

PAGE 100 | Nicolas Feuillatte, the champagne of the 21st Century

It is because of its partnership with great sailors that Nicolas Feuillatte champagne has criss-crossed many of the world's seas.

Very soon rugby, sailing and tennis were sponsored by the Nicolas Feuillatte brand. Christian Labit (RCNM) and Jean-Louis Jourdan (Stade Toulousain), former rugby players of the 2000's gather around Nicolas Feuillatte.

On the following page Raphael Nadal, winner of the Swedish Open in 2005 is presented with a jeroboam of Nicolas Feuillatte champagne.

Claims that the Champagne region is looking with optimism towards the new millennium, with booming sales of stunning wines grown on bountiful land would mean forgetting the lessons of the past. Consumer patterns do not live up to expectations forecast for 2000. Regrettably, this "return to normality" set the alarm bells ringing for only a small number of the most perceptive people.

2000-2010, a decade of paradoxes

Much like everywhere else things are momentarily on hold at the Centre Vinicole in 2000. Everyone is waiting on Sylvain Delaunois', the newly appointed president, realistic appraisal at the general meeting. There is a "return to normal consumer patterns and a significant reduction in sales linked to the stocks bought by the distribution circuits in 1998/1999[172] which remain unsold".

With his developer's mindset, Jean-Marc Pottiez pursues his marketing policies, forges new partnerships and develops the brand's links with the contemporary art world "given that we must stand out in an increasingly competitive market." "We have long-term ambitions for our brand, and we are determined to stand out from the crowd, Nicolas Feuillatte must set down the foundations of its communication policy, positioning itself firmly in the market and exploiting its uniqueness." The first publicity campaign is launched[173] in the somewhat flat market of 2000. The venture into the contemporary art world does not simply consist in "associating" an artist in residence with the brand for a year. It involves widening the scope to an international level, and includes participation in the reopening of the Centre Pompidou in Paris, the inauguration of Tate Britain and Tate Modern in London and several vernissages (MoMa in New York

172. These are stocks bought by the members at a higher market rate as requested by the board in preparation for the increased demands related to the celebrations of 2000. We know today that – as with other areas linked to lifestyles and associated with such celebrations – the momentous transition to this historic millennium did not live up to the profession's expectations.
173. See chapter "Boldness & Communication"

On 8th June 2004 Michel Desjoyeaux won the 12th Transat sur Geant at Boston. His victory much like the Route du Rhum won in 2003 was celebrated with Nicolas Feuillatte Brut.

and so on.). In addition to its connections with the art world, Nicolas Feuillatte champagne is also involved in regional and national level sport, supporting a range of disciplines including rugby, sailing and women's tennis. Moreover, a tour route is set up at Chouilly. Jean-Marc Pottiez sees the tour as an "innovation offering a credible alternative to the more traditional brands. It is a voyage into the heart of the operation enabling visitors to witness the way the grapes are vinified and to see the work of the winegrowers at first hand. It's not just about tasting the different blends". Works of art are displayed in the cellars "in a bid to forge closer links between the work of artists and the artisans making our wine and running the cellars". All this, as far as the Chief Executive Officer is concerned, is just the beginning.

The directors support their leader. Alain Robert believes that "the sales representatives work too quickly", warning the board that "if our cooperative members have the right to earn reasonably well, they do not have the right to loose money". As the new millennium approaches he embarks upon a new journey, "We must pass our knowledge on to younger people" says the prudent president of the Centre Vinicole, we're in a tough business, and it's not to be taken lightly!" Laziness? Bitterness? There's a bit of both without doubt for in addition to enjoying the success of the completion of the project, Alain Robert has not been able to lead this new business plan entirely successfully, which he regarded as his "great passion", and which was so dear to his heart. What he yearned to do was to develop the CVC's brand into a great and historic label[174]. True to the cause of "liberal cooperation", Alain Robert was to pursue his dream relentlessly.

---

174. The trading house that owned Mumm and Perrier-Jouët was subsequently owned in 1998 by Seagram's. The pension funds of the Texan Hicks Muse bought back this company in order to sell it to Allied-Domecq in 2002. In 2005 Mumm and Perrier-Jouët were bought by the Pernod-Ricard group.

"I constructed a framework in which our winegrowers could benefit from a capitalist system. I went to the COB headquarters to see how a shareholding company operated. I found it a little complicated, but I personally put in a lot of effort on the subject." It was his idea to turn his members into investing shareholders. In 1998 he approached Crédit Agricole Nord-Est, of which he was a director. He also worked on the brief with Indosuez, the investment bank owned by Crédit Agricole.

Crucially, people listened to him and the project was discussed at the highest level. "But the subject was to become highly contentious and my colleagues gave up on the idea. And that was the end of that", concluded Alain Robert who has his own opinions on why the project failed[175]. "I was completely fed up of the situation and it was then that I began to distance myself from the Centre."

But he did not distance himself from the board of directors, over whom he kept a vigilant eye. He appreciated many of Jean-Marc Pottiez' qualities but found it difficult to accept that he "did not fully let go of the breaks". Indeed he blocked them fully the day the developer presented him with the new project[176]. "In a bid to promote continued development of tours to the Centre, he wanted to build a pioneering tourist centre! He wasn't interested in investing in maintenance, and there was no money set aside to pay for it", recounts the former president.

"That is not entirely correct", Jean-Marc Pottiez argues, brandishing the file. Investments, floating capital and redemption funds had all been calculated by a professional company armed with relevant expertise, and a realistic estimate was made based on the number of visitors to the Centre which immediately made the venture profitable."

Winner of the Open Gaz de France in 2000, Serena Williams is handed a magnum of Nicolas Feuillatte by Jean-Marc Pottiez, director general of the Centre Vinicole, together with Jacques Girod, director general of Maison Richard.

175. The reasons behind why the project failed can be attributed to a powerful group of buyers who had concerns about a deal that had never been struck that was deemed to compromise the balance of powers within the champagne industry.
176. Jean-Marc Pottiez hoped with the "Nicolas Feuillatte tourist centre" "to achieve long term development of the brand".
177. *Les Échos,* September 2002. If Jean-Marc Pottiez refuses to question the figures relaid by the financial daily, he makes it clear however that he cannot be held responsible for "the increased stock levels" as a result of the sales forecast for 2000 (see footnote 172).

Sylvain Delaunois

Born in Épernay in 1949, Sylvain Delaunois joined the Centre Vinicole de la Champagne having been president of the Fleury-la-Rivière cooperative. He was appointed to the Board of Directors of the CVC in May 1998 and elected president in 2000. His wide ranging experience in the champagne industry and cooperatives operating at both regional and national level complements his work at the Centre Vinicole – Champagne Nicolas Feuillatte. He is responsible for enlarging the Centre's activities and subsequently marketing the Nicolas Feuillatte brand and achieving global recognition. Mindful of the inherent weaknesses in the balance of power between growers and buyers he has fought for equality and cooperation in the Champagne region, ensuring that the CV – CNF provides a credible alternative. Achieving long-term autonomy for the winegrowers and producing a high-quality product are the goals that are top of his agenda.

Alain Robert and the board of directors' refusal regarding the project is nevertheless categorical and he is even more concerned about this than the "essential" investments needed to develop the brand that began to weight heavily on the winegrowers who were becoming increasingly weighed down by the whole affair.

The net loss suffered in 2001 following the net profit divided by ten the year before, and faced with the scenario of a substantial increase in stocks and a net debt already 2 to 3 times greater that the company's equity meant the Centre Vinicole had to take a backward step", so financial reports surmise[177]. Jean-Marc Pottiez is thanked in early 2001 for adopting a strategy regarded by all concerned as too expansionist.

A new president is elected at the Centre Vinicole, taking over from Alain Robert a few months later. Sylvain Delaunois, a winegrower at Fleury-la-Rivière and president of his local cooperative, was appointed to the board of the Centre Vinicole in 1998. He had also been president of the Fédération des coopératives[178] since 1993. History repeats itself. Like his predecessors Henri Macquart and Serge Rafflin, the new incumbent hails from a cooperative and unionist background. An ardent defender championing the rights of winegrowers, he firmly believes in developing the Centre. It is not Sylvain Delaunois' intention to wipe the slate clean, but, armed with a wealth of experience acquired at both regional and national level[179], he goes on to shake up the organization radically in order to achieve his objectives. At his first general meeting in 2001 he pays homage to the work carried out by his predecessors before his arrival. In discussing the failures of 2000, he underlines that "Our progress in establishing the brand in the market place and promoting the right image has led to success in the market, proving that the measures taken were far from futile". "Yet we should not be resting on our laurels", and with the following statement revealing his ambiguity on the future, Sylvain Delaunois plays the moral card, "The management of our enterprise must be more rigorous. Our landscape is evolving and the influence held by buyers has never been stronger. We must strive for development with determination."

As far as Sylvain Delaunois is concerned, the Centre Vinicole must grow within stringent parameters in order to build a solid future for our members (and their families) without failing to address their requirements. The measures taken comply with the precepts of the cooperative movement[180]. Three weeks later, in March 1995, the board of directors appoints Dominique Pierre to the post of joint Chief Executive Officer in charge of relations at every level of the industry[181].

Sylvain Delaunois and Dominique Pierre have known each other for many years, and enjoy a relationship based on mutual respect. They work well together as a partnership.

178. He renounced his position as president of the Fédération that year in order to "dedicate himself fully to the Centre". He continues to be the Fédération's vice-president.
179. Sylvain Delaunois held several appointments in regional, national and international bodies. He is, amongst other positions, treasurer of the Haut Conseil de la coopération agricole (HCCA), member of the board of the Fédération régionale des coopératives agricoles Champagne Ardenne (FRCA), president of the legal and fiscal committee of the Confédération des coopératives vinicoles de France (CCVF), member of the national committee of INAO and was from 1995 to 1999 a member of the wine advisory board in Brussels.
180. When Alain Robert left, he claimed he had "Handed over the spirit of cooperation to the members".
181. Before being appointed to the Centre Vinicole, Dominique Pierre was responsible for the winegrowers' estates at the Comité interprofessionel du vin de Champagne (CIVC) between 1980 and 1995.

The partnership worked right from the start. The two men knew and respected each other well. Entirely in tune with one another, their appraisal of the situation was the same. Dominique Pierre did not beat about the bush when replying to a journalist asking him what his intentions were, "The previous spending policy was inadequate, with no concern for investment. Our objective now is to innovate by increasing production levels and boosting finances". This statement shows the eagerness of a president who applauds the "deep understanding shown by the board and heads of departments". The 2002 statistics speak for themselves, the Centre has redressed the fundamental issues, has regained control and is progressing well. So much so that turnover is 15% higher than 2001 and the commercial activity is growing at the same rate. In his report, Frédéric Burgun[182] underlines that "Healthy commercial activity linked to our desire to achieve long-term development has led to a 20% increase in added value over the year". The gross operating surplus has grown by 40% in the same period. The restructuring of the accounts has led to achieving greater autonomous financial control resulting in a spectacular increase of 213%. The net operating profit has grown from 2,709,000 euros in 2000 to more than 2,416,000 euros in two years, despite the unfavourable rate of exchange between the dollar and euro.

Sylvain Delaunois writes "Things have worked out very smoothly for the Centre Vinicole – Champagne Nicolas Feuillatte[183] in 2002". Dominique Pierre believes that this unprecedented success will encourage "our goal in achieving controllable growth, [….], and appreciable development of the Nicolas Feuillatte brand based principally on value rather than volume". In fact, 6,000,000 bottles were produced "and earmarked for all our markets in a bid to minimise areas of weakness". Inter-professional balance of power continues to be of primary concern in the region. Sylvain Delaunois states "the biggest buyers have different interests from the producers". The moment the president of the CV – CNF steps down from the presidency of the Fédération des coopératives vinicoles de la Champagne, "the winegrowers producing their own champagne account for 32% of champagne market. The growth of the cooperative movement since 1993 has enabled us to maintain the balance of power at a commercial level between winegrower and buyer, despite the winegrowers' decrease in the market share. The number of bottles produced by cooperatives has risen from 16,000,000 to nearly 25,000,000, representing a 56% increase, with some unions producing an average of 7 to 8,000,000 bottles per year. In commercial terms the journey undertaken by the cooperatives is even more remarkable as the average price of a bottle has also risen, proving that winegrowers can produce a strong and solid brand[184] within a cooperative environment". There is nothing belligerent in what Sylvain Delaunois has to say, despite his use of the term "balance of power". Unaggressively he reiterates to his CV – CNF members in 2002 gathered at the general meeting that "The cooperation movement offers a credible alternative that is in no way despotic in its desire to take control of our future".

The healthy balance sheet of 2002 goes from strength to strength in 2003 with sales of the Nicolas Feuillatte brand totalling 6,700,000, which equates to an approximate 8% rise. According to industry leaders, this increase exceeds all expectations which had been set at 2 to 3%. A rise in the retail price is in line with this growth, which can be summarised by a few figures: Nicolas Feuillatte champagne is the top selling brand in the hypermarkets and the second widest distributed, with a 5% market share. Export figures are highly encouraging, with an increase in sales of 16% equating to 2,700,000 bottles. US sales leap from 435,000 to

---

182. Frédéric Burgun was appointed as joint director general deptily Managing Director and finance in 2001.
183. The Centre Vinicole de la Champagne (CVC) is renamed the Centre Vinicole – Champagne Nicolas Feuillatte (CV – CNF) in 2001.
184. Source: FCVC.

an impressive 620,000, with the brand eager to follow in the footsteps of the great, historic brands firmly established on the market[185].

A beaming Sylvain Delaunois and Dominique Pierre stand side by side on the front cover of the accounts for 2004. There is clearly a deep understanding between the pair. Once again, the president affirms that "Our work has been achieved with the full cooperation of the board of directors and heads of department who together have worked towards a unified strategy". This is evidently the case when one takes a glance at the results. The increases are due to an improved contractual provision of grapes, proving the members' confidence in the policies instituted by the two partners at the helm of the Centre. Moreover, Dominique Pierre hails Nicolas Feuillatte's entry into the "top five" of the world's champagne houses, attaining the 7,000,000 mark of bottles sold, "which represents a tenfold increase over a ten year period[186]". The members and board are "in all modesty justifiably proud [of the importance of the Centre Vinicole – Champagne Nicolas Feuillatte] and of the economic role it plays in the industry[187]".

Increased value and buoyant international sales (with 44% attributed to the export market) boost everyone's confidence. Which is much needed in order to significantly reduce the fees paid to the buyers, a direct consequence of increased sales of the brand. A development strategy is very much on the cards for the CV – CNF which is eager to maintain "the highest standards of our products over the following years". In order to achieve this the Centre has to change the way it sells its assets. "Under the new contract, the bottles being made can be sold on site as can the must and base wines which have been vinified[188]." This led to a reduction in turnover of some 13,000,000 euros. The repercussions of this new way of collaborating with the champagne houses was phased out the following year and the "figures returned to normal[189]".

The Centre Vinicole develops apace with the encouraging harvests at the beginning of the decade. With the exception of 2001[190] mother nature is generous, presenting the cellar master with high quality grapes to vinify and it produces consistently good wines of exceptional quality. "Things could not be better."

Captain of the French national Rugby team, Fabien Pelous pictured here in 2004 with Dominique Pierre, Chief Executive Officer of the CV – CNF.

185. In 2000 only three brands sold tipped the 1,000,000 sales mark in the United States: Moët & Chandon, Veuve Clicquot-Ponsardin and G.-H Mumm.
186. 736,000 bottles of Nicolas Feuillatte champagne were sold in 1993. A free flow of exchange means that sales of other brands produced by the Centre Vinicole are on a downward turn (1,880,000 bottles). This is a reflection on the Centre's desire to promote the Nicolas Feuillatte brand first and foremost.
187. Sylvain Delaunois in his annual report of 2004.
188. Frédéric Burgun in his financial report of 2004.
189. Frédéric Burgun in his financial report of 2005.
190. "Fortunately, the reserve wines resulted in a decent BSA (blended brut)". Jean-Pierre Vincent.

The concept of forming an association between Nicolas Feuillatte and contemporary art took hold at the end of the 1990's. The idea took on a new dimension in 2002 with the inception of the Prix Nicolas Feuillatte for contemporary art. Published here are stills from a short film based on the theme of "Effervescence" made by German artist Marc Comes, winner of the 2004 prize.

The new management at the helm of the CV – CNF under president Delaunois and his board did not change the current development operations. If rigorous economic policies impinge upon Marketing and Communication strategies, then earlier pledges, some of which are reconsidered, are also re-integrated into the new system in a bid to rationalize and reinvest. In tackling new policies, communication will be "less intrusive but will encourage greater cohesion, and based on Nicolas Feuillatte brand values (authenticity, individuality, permanence, conviviality and vitality) and what it represents. Our aim is for consumers to share a sufficiently unified perception of the brand[191]."

"Our brand must be firmly etched in the consumers' mind", "Knock the nail on the head", these are the priorities of the director of sales and marketing at the beginning of the decade. The first advertising campaign is more successful than any other in promoting a champagne brand and in winning the approval of more than 70% of consumers it is the recipient of Paris's "Prix de l'affiche", repeating its success in 2003 and 2006. Nicolas Feuillatte focuses once again on contemporary art[192] – it enjoys exclusive presence at FIAC in 2002, snatching the coveted accolade from Pommery, and sponsors a number of sporting events in sailing, rugby and golf[193].

The commitment to research into quality is unwavering. The Centre's laboratory is awarded the COFRAC[194] accreditation, thereby obtaining official recognition of its technical competence. The Centre obtained the ISO 14001 certification[195] just a few months earlier, hailing the Centre's commitment to pursuing its environmental programme, the water treatment plant being a central focus of attention. The British Retail Consortium (BRC, version 3) commends the Centre for the quality and safety of its produce. The Centre Vinicole is "The first French enterprise to have been awarded this number of distinctions in recognition of its management systems[196]".

The Nicolas Feuillatte website – www.feuillatte.com – is much liked for its conceptual design and its content translated into both English and German.

As the Centre develops, so does its stature in the profession. The renewal of inter-professional agreements in 2004 reaffirms the Centre's solid credibility. The straightforward and profitable mechanisms involved in grape supplies are now indelibly linked to the meteoric success of the Nicolas Feuillatte brand, and owe much to the regulations

Very soon many of the world's greatest chefs conceived pairings with their dishes and Nicolas Feuillatte cuvées to demonstrate that they can be partnered by fine dining. To this end Fumiko Kono has concocted hitherto unexplored culinary associations with Jean-Pierre Vincent.

191. Laurent Davaine (director of commerce and marketing from 2001 to 2004) in the Annual Report of 2003.
192. See the illustration overleaf.
193. See chapter "Boldness & Communication".
194. COFRAC: COmité FRançais d'ACcréditation.
195. A certification awarded by the Association française pour l'Assurance Qualité (AFAQ).
196. The Report read out at the general meeting of 2001.

1 - Following in the footsteps of Olivier Roëllinger, winner of chef of the year 2005, seen here with Dominique Pierre at Paris' InterContinental, some of the world's greatest chefs have celebrated the qualities inherent in Nicolas Feuillatte champagne. Distinguished sommeliers, (-2) including Enrico Bernardo, winner of the finest sommelier in the world in 2004 (pictured here in the middle) and Olivier Poussier, the 1999 winner (pictured here on the left) are on the opposite page.

stipulated in former inter-professional contracts. It was president Delaunois who states unequivocally that the mechanisms "Are in harmony with unionist ideals".

2005 is a year that stands out in the history of the Centre Vinicole – Champagne Nicolas Feuillatte. The wine industry is going through tough times. Outside Champagne many wine regions face disaster, and operating in a region that is safe makes the board even more wary. Sylvain Delaunois emphatically calls for prudence to ensure that the appellation system continues to work successfully. Champagne's impeccable quality must be emphasised, a dynamic communication strategy pursued and a balance between controlled production and market demands struck. Yet in order for this to happen, greater cooperation from other partners and comprehensive analytical involvement is called for. It's an unrealistic dream. The president is doubtful: "Unfortunately", he writes in 2006, "I'm not convinced that in a positive economy promoting individualism and inward focus this can be achieved". This pessimism which time will tell if it is justified does not prevent the Centre from "building a new future", to coin the phrase frequently used by Dominique Pierre. The Centre must take a momentary pause and take stock of the situation "In order to ensure we are always on track" with the board's policies.

If five years ago, our first priority was to consolidate our financial foundations [….], much of what we set out to achieve has been realised over this period." A meditative director general ponders over increased supplies harvested from larger vineyards, a rise in the price of grapes, revivals in the market leading to a 7% increase in members' numbers, a facility undergoing constant development and, let it be clear, the formidable commercial success of the Nicolas Feuillatte brand verging on sales of 8,000,000 bottles. The brand is now exported to 75 countries and its value escalates by 13%. 2006 could conceivably be considered as a stepping stone towards a consolidation policy in line with the boards' desire to see beyond "the small pocket of prosperity of the champagne industry", anxious not to forget that "nothing is achieved without hard work". In an interview given in the Autumn of 2005, when the great sales manoeuvres of the preceding summer[197] were touched upon, Dominique Pierre stated that "The fundamental aim of financial groups is to make business. And the historic, family-owned Champagne houses are disappearing thick and fast and losing their human identity".

That is why, according to the board and heads of department, the Centre Vinicole has an important role to play in a Champagne market in metamorphosis. "The winegrowers, uncertain about future supply contracts tying them to certain brands, have declared their support of us". The plural "us" has no "royal we" connotations. He is willingly including his predecessors and refers on several occasions to his collaborators.

"Today Nicolas Feuillatte wants to achieve greater fame". The objective is to profit as much as possible from their magnificent winegrowing estates and state-of-the-art facility which nobly meet the needs of the gigantic enterprise the Centre has become[198]. The dream of the great distribution network is being chased. Sylvain Delaunois is not a man who minces his words. In an interview he simply states that "growth in sales is achievable by conquering the new export and large scale distribution markets[199]". Large scale distribution is a vague enough term. "Well, when he spoke of large scale distribution, I told him we should launch headlong into it", an animated Dominique Pierre recounts. The distribution circuit is ubiquitous, accounting for a 60% share in the French market alone. One simply cannot ignore it." Furthermore, many of France's most prestigious houses were part of the network, and this allegiance did not appear to influence consumers' mentalities. Nicolas Feuillatte is to suffer a further blow in 2005, and one that according to the Chief Executive Officer had been on the cards. Clearly, the quality of its champagnes was not called into question, in fact its wines had won no less than 50 distinctions and awards in 2004, inflating an already flattering list of prizes[200]. "We grew little by little as it was important to bear in mind that we were a relatively young brand."

Nicolas Feuillatte champagne celebrates its 30th birthday in 2006 and the opportunity to sum up what the brand has achieved is seized with open arms, as is the commitment to "position it firmly on the ladder of the "great" names in Champagne." The 2006 financial report signed by Sylvain Delaunois and Dominique Pierre states unequivocally that this is the best way "to achieve a justifiable income from bottles" made at the Centre Vinicole and guarantee "growing independence for our winegrowers". The director's reply to those judging these demands to be a little over ambitious is "No, it is realistic and necessary given that the environment in which we operate is in permanent flux."

The financial situation of the CV – CNF is for the time being reassuring. The balance sheet is healthy and in line with the Centre's net profits up by 27%. The sales revenue for Nicolas Feuillatte champagne on its own is nearly 1,500,000 euros. "Now is the time to tweak the brand's image", writes the Chief Executive Officer

---

197. Mumm and Perrier-Jouët in *Vins & Gastronomie*, Autumn 2005.
198. The CV–CNF was at the beginning of 2006 the largest winegrowers' union, representing the interests of 5,000 winegrowers, equating to approximately 7% of the appellation zone.
199. In *Vignerons coopérateurs*, Nobember 2006.
200. 9 gold medals and top class ratings in the international guides.

in a special edition of Magazine. In the opinion of the president of the Union des Maisons de Champagne[201], the brand's image has "much in common with those of the champagnes made by the Union des Maisons de Champagne". The man with fountain pen in hand believes that the Nicolas Feuillatte brand "has a great and long term international future ahead, and is an great asset in the champagne world". This acknowledgement is a tribute bestowed by the historic champagne houses and is regarded by everyone at Chouilly as a recognition of their achievements[202].

Do we need to look for a hidden meaning behind the Centre Vinicole – Champagne Nicolas Feuillatte's agreeing to host four shows given by the Cirque Pinder in June 2006? As far as the directors are concerned it is done to foster conviviality amongst its members. The events could be interpreted differently. Much like what goes on under its famous big top, Chouilly also found itself juggling several balls in the air, performing acrobatics, conquering mother nature and proving the organisation's ability to put on a sparkling show to the delectation of the public during which champagne lovers of the Nicolas Feuillatte brand could partake of a sip. Not only were the 7,700 spectators toing and froing along the terraces, thrilled to be watching the show, they more importantly were taking part in a festive occasion celebrating the success of this young brand, a great actor in the great champagne arena.

"2007 was a good year. 2008, in global terms was highly satisfactory …" In retrospect, in reading what president Delaunois had to say, one could rightly assume that there were no hiccups in 2007 and 2008. What happened was nothing other than a positive progression in the wake of the preceding years. This indeed was the case in terms of turnover and productivity. The financial situation is solid, and a record 27,300,3000 bottles are produced in 2007[203]. In the very same year Nicolas Feuillatte champagne tipped the 9,000,000 mark in bottles sold in France, consolidating its ranking amongst the front running champagne brands (no. 1 in France and top 4th in the world)[204]. "Our financial situation is enviable", affirms Frédéric Burgun[205] as Nicolas Feuillatte takes its place amongst the Top 5 champagne brands in the world.

And most fortuitously, as the financial markets have been rocky for several months, starting in the Spring of 2007 with the collapse of the American housing market (subprime[206]) which led to a domino effect of failures. It was because of financial globalization that the economic turmoil in America spread to countries whose banks who had handed out mortgages to Americans.

Sylvain Delaunois and Dominique Pierre alerted their members at the general meeting held in May 2008 to a year "which may well be marked by national and international perturbations and a recession of varying magnitude depending on each country, which will inevitably lead to reduced buying power, which in turn will implicate consumer patterns". These warnings are not nearly as explicit in the forecasts for the following year: "2009 will be a difficult year …"

In August 2008 because Dominique Pierre forecasts a reduction in sales throughout the region, his colleagues are maligning him because of this gloomy prognosis. Yet he is proved right by the facts. England and the US are the first to collapse. These two markets are the second and third most important for the Nicolas Feuillatte brand and the epidemic spreads to Europe. Given the possible implications, the CV- CNF board of directors concur that only essential investments can be made.

From early 2009 there is a marked fall in sales with

201. Yves Bénard, quoted previously.
202. See Chapter "An Eye to the Future?"
203. This figure is close to the 27 million bottles sold by the entire Champagne region in … 1949.
204. In 2007, according to Jocelyne Dravigny, president of the coopératives vinicoles de la Champagne, they sold 31,000,000 bottles of their brands, as quoted in 13th June 2008 edition of *La Marne agricole*.
205. Deputy Managing Director, in his report of May 2007.
206. High risk mortgage loans given in the United States after September 11.

The Centre Vinicole hosted four shows performed by the Cirque Pinder conceived specially for Nicolas Feuillatte champagne in June 2006. Not only were the 7,700 spectators toing and froing along the terraces, thrilled to be watching the show, they more importantly were taking part in a festive occasion celebrating the success of this young brand, a great actor in the great champagne arena.

consequences for the whole of the profession. Shipments had fallen by 4.8% in 2008.

"It's not as bad as we'd expected!", so say the press releases. The Comité interprofessionnel des vins de Champagne remains positive in its outlook. After all "with 322,400,000 bottles dispatched, the industry figures are better than those of 2006 (312,700,700)[207]." Ghislain de Montgolfier, co-president of the CIVC notes that "Production figures are nothing short of brilliant" and "in any case, this 4.8% reduction was necessary as we were progressing too quickly". Yves Dumont, president of Laurent-Perrier Development, is the director of economic forecasting at the CIVC which is fully geared up to anticipate the hazards of the market "and will not react six months or a year later[208]".

As usual, because of their inter-dependence, statistics are misleading. The French market is reassuring, with 181,200,000 bottles sold (down by 3.6%), and has limited the effects of the crisis effectively. The winegrowers also came out on top despite the forecast financial turmoil, with shipments increasing by 1%. But these results need to be put into perspective with the volume of champagne dealt with by the three principle actors of the profession: 210,000,000 plus bottles produced by the champagne houses, nearly 80,000,000 by the winegrowers themselves and 30,000,000 produced by cooperatives. Clearly the 20% plunge in the American

207. Quoted in *L'Union* and *L'Ardennais* on 10th February 2009.
208. This is what Patrick Le Brun claims, who at the time was president of the SGVC and co-president of the CIVC.

markets has not had the same impact in France. On the other hand, it would be somewhat unpalatable to be self congratulatory because of the 50% increase in sales in China (with sales reaching the 1,000,000[209]) which counterbalance the deficit in sales of several million bottles in the English and American markets, though this is a derisory, if not deceptive, compensation. Lastly, it is important to be in agreement with what's written in the press releases. For example a bottle that's left the cellar is not necessarily one that's been sold. For those running the accounts department, what's needed are spending cuts. "The bottles produced by us were as far as we're concerned sold", Dominique Pierre tirelessly repeats". This desire to make a distinction between the bottles leaving the cellars and those sold continues. With its 5.5% deficit Nicolas Feuillatte fares better than the other cooperatives who register a 5.7% fall in 2008. The Centre's sales, and likewise those of its contemporaries operating in Champagne, plunge significantly in the North American market. Yet because its champagne is sold in 96 countries[210], Nicolas Feuillatte is ranked 7th amongst exported brands and is in the top three in terms of sales, with net results of 10,200,000 euros, a 7% increase on 2007. Turnover increases by 4% (193,000,000 euros). In terms of commercial activity, the increase in sale prices compensates for the last quarter's deficit. The general meeting of May 2009, attended by Philippe Mangin, president of France's Coop[211], is conducted amidst an air of tranquillity.

Yet, the hardest times are to follow. Clearly, the Champagne region has battled with, and overcome, more than its fair share of crises, some linked to international circumstances, others the consequences of political-professional disagreements. Yet this one has drastic and, more than likely, long-term implications. The changes in consumers' behaviour are a real cause for concern within this extreme environment. Prudence is called for, not passivity and lethargy. It is important within this climate to resist the temptation of selling bottles at cut price. "We are not interested in scrambling about for inappropriate special offers, as they would discredit our product which would have dire implications on future sales[212]", Dominique Pierre states.

Yet as far as his board in concerned, the Centre Vinicole should set other aims in order to deal with the crisis. The retail cost for each bottle should be set at a decidedly lower, yet realistic level, in line with the other champagne houses operating in the luxury market.

The measures taken by the Member States[213] in the Spring of 2009 are a drop in the ocean as far as the CV – CNF goes, particularly as the global financial system needs regulating. Recovery is slow and the consumer buying patterns are stagnant this year.

The number of bottles leaving the cellar are 9.1% (293,300,000) down on the previous year[214]. Sales remain stable in France but plunge by 17.4% in Europe and 25.1%in the rest of the world. However, the fact that there has been an increase on the number of bottles leaving the cellars in the last two months of 2009, lead the profession to believe that the worst is over for the champagne sector. But is it possible to predict what the future holds?

---

209. 896,000 bottles in 2008.
210. The number of countries invoiced has nearly tripled in eight years.
211. See Chapter "An Eye to the Future?"
212. Quoted in *La Marne agricole* of 13th February 2009.
213. The G20 met in London on 2nd April 2009.
214. These sums were communicated by the CIVC on 5th February 2010.

A recent survey revealed that 4 out of every 10 champagne bottles bought in France were Nicolas Feuillatte. The brand achieved second place in 2009 in terms of customer loyalty and in that very same year saw a 13% increase in new consumers.

1 - 2. The open tanks of the Centre Vinicole – Champagne Nicolas Feuillatte await the ritual offering from the presses. These stainless steel tanks today collectively have a 30,000,000 liter capacity.

The strong position Nicolas Feuillatte holds in the French and foreign markets and the brand's distinguished reputation testify to the esteem in which the brand is held by consumers and professionals alike. This widespread recognition entails the fulfilment of certain obligations. Having achieved rapid development and consolidation, what is the Centre Vinicole's next objective? Amidst global instability, it must show courage and determination when faced with uncertainty.

An Eye to the Future?

The first decade of the third millennium[215] is full of contradictions for the Centre Vinicole Champagne – Nicolas Feuillatte, but it is also one in which the brand receives unprecedented recognition, which could not be bettered. Clearly the precious gold medals and high rankings have done much to promote victories of the Nicolas Feuillatte cuvées in international competitions[216]. The rewards are so numerous that they have for some time filled an entire large hall. The line of trophies could be seen by all the visitors to the Centre. It is today unnecessary to indulge in this topic of conversation.

---

215. See Chapter "2000-2010, A decade of paradoxes".
216. This catalogue of success refers to the first three years of the decade. The Palmes d'Or, Millésimes, Grands Crus and Brut GD were awarded gold medals. The Brut GD won gold medals at Moscow's Vinnaya Carta Open (2008), the Concours mondial de Bruxelles (2009) and Vinalies internationales (2010). In one way or another, the entire Nicolas Feuillatte range is worthy of recognition by some of the world's most demanding experts.

Yet it was not that long ago when the cellar master said "Sooner or later Nicolas Feuillatte champagne is going to have to be taken more seriously". If the profession chooses to ignore this (and that's fair enough) they still believe the company is a success. When one day an amiable cellar master colleague said to Jean-Pierre Vincent "You know, what you're doing is great!", it was without doubt one of the best compliments he could have wished for professionally.

Former president of the Centre Vinicole Alain Robert recalls "The product's quality was right there from the very start and has been consistently fine. The quality remained intact even when the boat rocked. The calibre of our wines made at Chouilly has never been called into question."

But these suppositions are hard to dismiss and not everyone can be part of the circle of top brands. A rich heritage is a precondition of access to the alliance[217], and this remains a sore point with everyone at Nicolas Feuillatte. Jean-Pierre Vincent expostulates by making an artistic analogy, comparing the Louvre with its Pyramid "Housed in Paris' museum is a collection of ancient art. We are like its Pyramid, new, but fully integrated with the historic collection." He adds, smiling craftily "It's through the Pyramid you get into the collection".

"Nicolas Feuillatte is the youngest of the great brands", says the journalist Michel Bettane. "It owes its success to the board's pragmatism. Founded on the finest champagne traditions, it has evolved according to consumer trends and tastes. It is the universal champagne of our time".

Show business personalities like Arnaud Delbarre[218] first discovered Nicolas Feuillatte champagne Johnny Hallyday and Michel Sardou were touring, "I was immediately struck by the freshness of the Brut Réserve Particulière", finding the brand had "similarities with the Olympia, most notably its ability to discover new talents[219]".

High quality grapes are an essential ingredient in champagne. It is down to the 4,500 or so members spread across the vineyards of the Champagne wine growing region that the tanks of le Centre Vinicole – Champagne Nicolas Feuillatte are replete with the finest crus from Montagne de Reims, Côte des Blancs, Vallée de la Marne and Côte des Bars.

217. The youngest of the great brands, Taittinger and Laurent Perrier, have been in existence since the mid 20th century. They can in fact boast a longer heritage, such as that of maison Fourneaux which was founded in 1734 and bought by Pierre Taittinger in 1932.
218. Arnaud Delbbarre has been director general and artistic director of Paris's Olympia since 2002.
219. The director general of the Olympia is referring here to the Prix Jeune Espoir Nicolas Feuillatte and more generally to the brand's involvement with contemporary art.

In 2002 Jim Galtieri[220] asserts that amongst the champagne brands he knows "Nicolas Feuillatte is the only one facing the future with confidence. It is the brand most synonymous with the 21st century, and in terms of its quality/price ratio they've hit the nail on the head. It has incredible potential".

Very soon many of the world's greatest chefs work with Nicolas Feuillatte cuvées, attesting to the product's successful partnership with fine dining[221]. However the sales figures are the best indicator of the product's enduring quality. One can't simply skirt over sales figures of 10,000,000 bottles and consumers' won't be deceived for long. A recent study shows that four out of ten champagne bottles bought in France are Nicolas Feuillatte. In 2009 the brand came second in a survey on consumer fidelity and in the same year 13% of those buying the champagne were new to the brand[222]. Now that's a tribute! From then on, with its 7% share in the champagne market, Nicolas Feuillatte is regarded as an industry heavyweight, as is the cooperative movement it owes its origins to.

"Our fledgling enterprise just grew and grew and we've seen the balance of power within the champagne market evolve as the years go by", stated Monsieur Jacques Houdard in 1987, vice-president of the general council of la Marne[223].

"The Champagne region is the only wine area to see its winegrowers increase in numbers since 1970 to the present day", states Sylvain Delaunois, unperturbed by this fact. "It's down to the fact that our predecessors understood that success and wealth should be enjoyed by everyone." In his opinion the success shared by all concerned was as a result of the institution of formalised inter-professional practices and the balance of power struck between the winegrowers and buyers[224]. He concurs with Paul Bergeot[225] who in the early 1980's stated that it is "a pointless exercise to look beyond the region for reasons behind the secret of champagne's success. It's all down to the appellation d'origine, allegiance between the great brands and winegrowers, quality assurance policies, and the buyers' dynamic commercial strategies. If any of these conditions were to disappear, the system would collapse". So, how are things looking three decades on? In 2008 Dominique Pierre noted that "The agreements previously set up in Champagne are no longer viable today; fifteen years ago everyone working in the industry was from the region. Today, we're dealing with financial groups with diverse interests and new boundaries have to be set[226]".

The CV – CNF is the leading cooperative union in Champagne and has attained economic well being. It has retained little of the original cooperative ethos which offered a credible alternative to an increasingly contentious economic system. No-one will be surprised to learn that Michel Rocard believed in social economy. "It took forty years of hard work to establish the statute and organizational framework", he wrote in 2007. "I believe the heart of the problem lay in changing the established laws and rules of the enterprise. The cooperative did not belong to outsiders funding the project; it was made of people who earned a living by sharing out the work in this economic venture[227]."

220. Jim Galtieri, president of Pasternak Wine Imports in the United States. After merging with Martin Sinkoff Wines in 2001 the company now represents in excess of 120 distributors across the U.S. Market. It was when Martin Sinkoff discovered Nicolas Feuillatte champagne at the 1995 VINEXPO that he decided to sell it in the United States. Today, the Michel company is the distributor of Nicolas Feuillatte in the United States.
221. Pierre Gagnaire, Alain Dutournier, Jean-Pierre Vigato, Philippe Augé, Jean-Marc Banzo and Christian Étienne are just some of the many and great chefs of international renown, some of which have already been cited, who continue to create dishes that are eminently accompanied by Nicolas Feuillatte.
222. The survey was carried out in 2009 by the Nielsen World Panel.
223. Speaking at the Centre Vinicole's general meeting in 1987.
224. *La Marne agricole* (March 2009), interviewed by Hugues Fourment.
225. *Champagne: la coupe est pleine*, written by Paul Bergeot, COFICOM, 1980.
226. *La Marne agricole*, 10th October 2008.
227. Le Nouvel Observateur. Former Prime Minister (1988 – 1991), Michel Rocard has been a Member of the European Parliament since 1994.

What was more surprising but nevertheless a politico-economic gesture was the encyclical letter of Pope Benedict XVI Caritas in Veritas, signed on 29th June 2009 in which the pontiff wholeheartedly endorses the development of the cooperative movement. "It is most opportune that organizations involved in production keen to pursue mutual and social goals can make their mark on the market and develop alongside private companies geared towards increasing profit margins and the wide range of public enterprises existing throughout the world."

A director of the cooperative movement and, president of France's Coop, Philippe Mangin, asks the question "Can one really treat agricultural raw materials as financial assets?" He has put forward a new concept, "cooperative capitalism", which is way to "promote economic efficiency with the collaboration of human ressources[228]".

But at the end of the day, can we with this formula face up to financial crises more effectively?

With the total sum of its activities, the CV – CNF closes 2009 with a turnover of 174,400,000 euros, a diminution of 9.7%. In refusing to lower its prices in the difficult economic climate and maintaining value more than volume, the CV – CNF is not tempted by short-term gain, opting for greater brand exposure. And this for the board is done in total respect for the consumer.

In every crisis the French wine industry has faced, the independent producers have achieved greater autonomy from traders and the cooperative movement but nevertheless they collectively account for 65% of the winegrowers' sales outlets. The CV – CNF is not immune to this trend. In 2009 it gave its members fewer bottles instead of payment and this led to an inflation of already heavy stocks because of a decrease in direct sales. The president's concern in 2010 was his opinion the certain cuvées would benefit from prolonged ageing in the cellars but the change in policy could have detrimental consequences on some champagnes. In the long run, prolonged ageing might encourage an evolution in the champagne's taste that consumers may find displeasing.

History has shown that this secondary phenomenon is reversed at the onset of economic recovery. The new technical armoury of a unified cooperative guaranteeing the unmistakable quality of its products and the financial benefits for its members are just some of the arguments in favour of a rapid return to the cooperative movement. These instinctive behavioural patterns do not satisfy Sylvain Delaunois who hopes that "the members' decision to show their allegiance to the Centre Vinicole shall continue to be taken in full conscience, and that factors other than the cost of grapes are taken into consideration". Following on from this observation, the president is delighted by the social evolution brought about by the cooperative. And it is because of it that "the winegrower has risen from his status as a farmer". One of the Centre's last pioneers Jean Deliège states in more prosaic terms that "the crisis did us a lot of good as winegrowers were better equipped to face reality[229]".

The statisticians of the CIVC[230] were over the moon about the healthy figures of the first quarter of 2010. 49,200,000 bottles had left the Centre's cellars, echoing the results of 2005. In analyzing the sector's principal economic indicators, the team estimated the deliveries to be made over the year. An attainable projected figure for the number of bottle leaving the Centre was set at a total of 310,000,000, a decidedly lower figure than those of 2007 and 2008. The wine region of Champagne, suffered losses of 700,000,000 euros. Analyses carried out on previous crises revealed that "it takes about six years to recover fully from a crisis". Sometimes more, when one goes back to 1990.".

228. Philippe Mangin speaking at the French Coop congress on 10th November 2009.
229. Interviewed by the author on 19th January 2010.
230. This working group became the Economic and Market Committee in 2010.
231. Approximately 150% on champagne (Source: CV – CNF).

> Sold in nearly 100 countries, the aims of Nicolas Feuillatte champagne in 2015 are to dispatch 11 million bottles from its store room. With the brand's firm positioning in the European, US, Australian and Japanese markets, the company is keen to capitalise on its already rapid growth in such divers markets as Russia, China, India and Brazil.

After every crisis everyone involved in the Champagne industry tries to anticipate future problems, with representatives from each sector fighting for their cause. With a limit set on supplies because of the renewable bilateral agreements with the winegrowers, the great champagne houses, increase their portfolio of vineyards and purchase plots outside the region. The CV – CNF does not need to recourse to these measures because of the increasing number of members joining the cooperative. The Centre could rely on steady growth in terms of its supplies strategy. It is reasonable to assume that the number of champagne bottles made at Chouilly can increase. In fact, president Delaunois sets a target of 11,000,000 Nicolas Feuillatte bottles for 2015. "Our brand has enormous potential and the only thing that can hold it back is the market", he argues. "As the top selling champagne brand in France it can indeed infiltrate the market even more, and as the world's third top selling brand there's scope for improvement at international level. We must implement both a strong commercial service and a redevelopment plan".

The brand's market analysts all believe that of all the emerging export markets, the most promising, and way ahead of China, is India. Sales would today be far greater if no tax were applied by the Indian state on imported products[231]. Nevertheless this huge country is a market to be developed "As champagne is part and parcel of its Anglo Saxon culture", explains Dominique Pierre. Brazil is seen as too volatile and the banks' coverage inadequate. The growth in the markets of Eastern Europe at the beginning of the decade slowed down appreciably after the crunch at the end of the decade. In general terms it is only fair to say that the leap in export figures widely reported in the press needs putting into perspective. Particularly when it comes to Russia. A 100% increase should always be compared to a base value. For example for Nicolas Feuillatte, starting with an initial export figure of 500,000 which then leaps up to nearly 1,000,000 is remarkable but, in absolute terms, this growth should be viewed in relative terms.

In the 1990's the directors of the Centre Vinicole did not dismiss the idea of external development. It was at this time that plans were made for takeover bids and mergers, attractive propositions offering access to new markets and complementary outlets for product lines. First to be approached was the CRVC who owned the Jacquart brand. "We handled it well as what we were dealing with was another group of cooperatives", explains Sylvain Delaunois, who at the time was on the board of directors and was aware of the fact that the team at the top of the CRVC was leaving." However, at the time, everyone was sceptical about the merger. The potential power of the merger made the unions quake with fear. The project fell through and the executives were highly disappointed. Subsequently advanced talks were held with Lanson. "We were on the verge of signing off the deal, but the Lanson directors called it off at the last minute", president Delaunois continues. A final bid was made by Alain Robert, but that failed too[232].

If external expansion is no longer part of today's agenda, Sylvain Delaunois confirms that "the idea has not however been entirely dropped". "The CV – CNF is open to potential acquisition[233]".

For the time being, the future of the Centre Vinicole lies in its brand. "It's essential for the brand to maintain its Top 5 status", says Dominique Pierre. When people talk about champagne, it's Nicolas Feuillatte we want them to be talking about. We want the brand to be synonymous with great champagne." In fact, continues the Chief Executive Officer of the CV – CNF, "it must make the transition from being recognised as a leading brand to achieving global fame".

A unique and highly individual communication strategy continues to be adopted today in order to achieve this entirely realistic goal. "Nicolas Feuillatte has a duty to champion its uniqueness and must have the courage to maintain its image intact, and the poise to persevere in its message communicating its success." These words are uttered by Pierre Berville[234],

Sylvain Delaunois, president of the CV – CNF states "There's yet more scope for the Centre to grow. As an economic enterprise it has a duty to safeguard the highest standards in the industry".

the inspired creator behind the wild animal themed campaign. Nicolas Feuillatte spends little on publicity, all the more reason for making its message loud and clear[235]. The 2010 Nicolas Feuillatte publicity campaign is a case in point. Nevertheless, it is no substitute for widespread communication propagated by the profession – which is a rare phenomenon indeed, as wished for by Sylvain Delaunois[236]. One cannot talk enough about champagne. For Dominique Pierre the success enjoyed today by the Centre Vinicole is due to the quality of its products, its empathy in its human relations and the way, it maximises the potential of the local terroir. It is for these three reasons that the Centre can look forward to a bright future. "There's still scope for further expansion at the Centre. It is essential we develop economically and maintain the highest standards in the industry", confirms Sylvain Delaunois", whilst always bearing in mind the balanced relationship between winegrower and buyer.

232. Approximately 150% on champagne (Source: CV – CNF).
233. Approximately 150% on champagne (Source: CV – CNF).
234. Interviewed by the author on 6th May 2010. See Chapter "Boldness & Communication" regarding the adertising campaigns.
235. It is worth noting that the champagne house that invests most in ad campaigns is still spending a relatively small amount on publicity.
236. The last adertising campaign run by the CIVC for champagne was in the 1980's.

Back in 2003 when Pascal Ferat[237] addressed the general meeting of the Fédération des coopératives, he predicted that "sales made by the winegrowers have reached their ceiling in distribution terms and that winegrowers' future development is in the hands of the cooperative movement". Assuring winegrowers' independence and inter-professional balance of power is an abiding objective. As the largest cooperative in Champagne, the CV – CNF plays a crucial part in achieving these aims. "Our successes to date should attract the support of winegrowers and should guarantee the long-term implementation of a system based on common interest and added value", the directors say. Aware of their needs, Pascal Ferat said "I hope that the winegrowers will seize full control of Nicolas Feuillatte champagne and that they will become shareholders reaping the benefits of dividend payments".

The call for the appellation district to be enlarged provokes a comment from president Delaunois. "We must carry this through as in order to develop our activities and brand we will have new margins for manoeuvre in terms of supplies at our disposal". The project to extend the appellation district is nevertheless put on hold in accordance with the regulations on plantation.

He moreover affirms that "the sustainability of family-run vineyards could be attained by achieving greater control at grass root level and this will lead to greater harmony in the sector[238]". The future success of the CV – CNF depends on another factor: distribution. "It's the minefield of the future! Our success will depend on the strength of our networks. But on the other hand we run the risk in operating within these mighty networks of becoming soulless and in order for this not to happen, the champagne industry must maintain its independence". And Dominique Pierre is insistent on this point.

Within the company, Nicolas Feuillatte, a fully satisfied octogenarian, knows full well that his name is now definitively etched in the history of champagne. Ambassador to the brand, he was succeeded by his nephew Éric, who as natural incumbent was duly appointed at general meeting on 12th May 2010. In performing this gesture the founder of the brand has symbolically bequeathed his estate to the next generation. Regarding the directors of the Centre, they will continue their work until the conclusion of their term of office and contract. They took over from their seniors, and likewise the younger generation will take over from them. Yet whatever the future holds for the president/Chief Executive Officer duo, it will be certainly be a partnership that, by agreement with the members and with their best intentions at heart, will continue the work of the enterprise cast in a strong cooperative mould, with phenomenal and fifty-year way over the continued balance of power in the Champagne region.

Predestined to excellence, the Centre must, declares Sylvain Delaunois, "Be able to continue to put its quality products on the market and draw benefit from its productive capacity and promote the pre-eminence of our brands and Champagne as a whole".

237. Pascal Ferat was at the time president of the FCVC (see footnote 134).
238. *Vignerons coopérateurs* (November 2006).

This work by Tanguy Loyzance, the 2006 artist in residence, called *Dream Travel* propels Nicolas Feuillatte into the world. It presents a bold image based on solid goals.

Champagne cooler created by the designer Christian Ghion. The artist began working with the Nicolas Feuillatte brand in 2001 and in that time has created a number of objects for it, including the *Cocoon* champagne bucket. He is also responsible for redesigning the Espace Nicolas Feuillatte in Paris.

PART THREE:
GREATER GOALS

The Cooperative's aims – supplies and allegiance to its winegrowing members, intelligent price control and its product's image of authenticity – are backed up by an exceptional state-or-the-art facility which is inextricably linked to a political ethos geared towards sustainability.

Yet what would this facility be without the men running it? One of the most important members of staff is the cellar master. The quality of the Centre's cuvees depends on him and his team. Savoir faire in making excellent champagne is all well and good, but knowing how to make them is even better. Importantly, the CV – CNF has developed a bold communication strategy that is both expansive and of universal scope.

The Nicolas Feuillatte signature, with its strong links to cellar masters across the globe, is a permanent feature of wine merchants' display cabinets and high end eateries.

The superb facility ranks as one of the Centre's greatest achievements. Those behind the initial project had the courage to look into a future fraught with uncertainties, and those following in the footsteps of these pioneers had the ability to adapt to an environment in constant flux. Everyone rose to the challenge, reacting in a highly responsible way. Today's steadfast commitment to sustainable development is very much in tune with the spirit in which the Centre was founded.

Given that it is an important component of research into the product's optimal quality, president Rafflin declared in 1984 that "We will rely more and more on sophisticated machinery". And he was proved right in the years that ensued.

An avant-garde facility

"Here and now, in 1972, all we've got are plots of land." This statement caused a stir amongst the members and heralded a series of plans made for the site over several years. In effect, it must have been difficult even for the veteran staff of the Centre Vinicole to picture what the slopes of Chouilly look like now with their succession of buildings fronted by vast parking lots and asphalt paved gangways. The pervading air of austerity is momentarily disrupted during the harvest period by the toing and froing of tanker lorries transporting the must coming from the numerous pressing centres scattered throughout the region.

All we've got are plots of land … in fact, that was to be the case only up until the Spring of 1972. In just a few months the constructions were beginning to loom out of the ground. Initially the site consisted of two separate buildings comprising four tank halls in front of which were several weighbridges, three cellars and an inter-connecting technical operations room. These two buildings were of modest proportions and

1 - 2. The laboratory has since the beginning of the Centre been of primary concern to those that set up the cooperative. And it was only a few years later that a second laboratory (the intercoopératif) saw the light of day. Members' samples can be analysed very efficiently, and at no extra cost, at any time of the year. With it the Centre Vinicole re-iterates its vocation as a facility operating at the service of the champagne industry.

have been largely swallowed up by today's complex of gigantic magnitude. As far as the pioneers of the Centre were concerned, they were two magnificent buildings with a 25,000 hectolitre storage capacity. Year after year, with the bulldozers and concrete mixers being a permanent fixture, the site got larger with the addition of new buildings, encroaching upon and eating up the surrounding land. The office space was extended in 1987, in 1988 the laboratory was enlarged, 1989 saw the opening of its first shop, in 1991 the quota of cellars reached to 23 and 2001 saw the first year of the construction of the water treatment plant.

But the first visitors to step inside the precinct constructed for them only saw a fraction of the Centre Vinicole's site which is today spread across 12 hectares and consists of vast tanks filled to the brim, cellars built on several levels, mechanically operated technical operating rooms, a warehouse and dispatch halls … A processing unit of gigantic proportions respecting champagne's nostalgic image of old. The care with which this king of wines is made continues to be impeccable and most encouragingly, because the vinification processes are constantly monitored, the level of care continues to develop. Dominique Pierre defines this industrial facility thus "Technology at the service of quality and tradition".

This is amply recognised by the agro-alimentary trade magazine *L'Usine nouvelle*, which nominated the Centre Vinicole – Champagne Nicolas Feuillatte as "Manufacturing plant of the Month" in 2009. The term "manufacturing plant" is an emotive phrase for champagne professionals and within the context of what they consider to be a false argument, the Chief Executive Officer declares once and for all, "It's semantics. Let's forget about the stereotypical image of champagne. It's great that we still have artisans working in the profession, but our development has led to traceability in the food industry, and that's important when you remember that we have a 7% share in the champagne market[239]". In short, champagne is an artisan product made with industrial means.

239. This declaration featured in a letter for internal circulation within CER France.

3 - 4 - 5. Champagne is an artisan product made by the incessant industrial machinations of an armoury of sophisticated equipment at the Centre Vinicole – Champagne Nicolas Feuillatte. The crystalline clinks of the bottles ring out in unison with the metallic whirrings of the conveyor belt. Today, as has always been the case, the tinkling bottles follow their unchanging route.

The resounding and incessant whirrings of the multi-tasking technology within this manufacturing plant ring out. Some of the equipment metronomically riddles the stacked bottles with balletic precision. Other equipment catches the muzzled bottles ten at a time, twists them round effortlessly, drops them into a refrigerated tank and after ejecting an ice cube of impurities and topping up the bottles immediately[240] with sleight of hand taking the chance observer unawares uncorks and re-corks them. Here the bottles have been pursuing their unchanging path for years. Once muzzled, capped in gold and bedecked in their armoury, the bottles packed in cases of six lay patiently waiting in the dispatch area before their final voyage transports them to one of the 96 countries in which Nicolas Feuillatte champagne is enjoyed.

The statistics speak volumes and are indicative of the production capacity of the Centre Vinicole – Champagne Nicolas Feuillatte.

The tank hall is equipped with stainless steel, thermo-regulated vats with a 304,000 hectolitre capacity, 20,000 bottles are filled an hour, 100,000,000 bottles can be stocked at any given point in time, 480 gyropalettes riddle 500,000 bottles a week. 9,000 bottles are chain-disgorged per hour and 9,000 bottles are labelled per hour. And mechanical boxing machines place the bottles in their cases.

240. In order to disgorge the deposits, the bottle neck is plunged into a glycol bath with a -25° temperature. The bottles are then uncorked and the deposits are easily ejected because of the 6 kg of pressure accumulated during the secondary fermentation.

Wood is rarely found in the metallic universe of the tank hall. In fact, the only wood present in the tank hall is found in the wood barrels used for partially ageing the remarkable cuvée 225.

This production facility of exceptional capacity allows the CV – CNF to profit from a "fully automated production system that assures our products' quality". The cellars themselves today have storage capacity for 100,000,000 bottles. Improvement measures implemented consistently since the early 1970's have been carried out in a bid to uphold the intentions of the pioneers of the Centre, so much so that the equipment today eminently responds to the demands made by the market and its members.

As the Centre has grown, so has the number of members increased. Today there are more than 200 women and men working on the site. Staff numbers have grown organically, with some posts filling out and others doubling up. The directors have appointed deputies to assist the Finance and Technical Directors. The Technical Director had before 1996 been responsible for production, but that was all to change with the appointment of Thierry Gomérieux. Not long afterwards it was the cellar master who became in charge of liaison in the industry, succeeding Dominique Pierre who in turn was promoted to the position of Chief Executive Officer. Because of their total respect for the champagne terroir and as they were very early on concerned about impact on the environment, the Centre adopted sustainable practices[241]. It was within this framework that the Centre Vinicole de la Champagne embraced a pioneering policy by applying its "quality charter" as advised by the profession in 1987, which by incredible coincidence was the year when the international agreement for the protection of the environment was signed. Chouilly's efforts in this regard rapidly gain ground[242], resulting in being awarded various ISO certifications in the 1990's, in addition to its implementation of the 14001 environmental management standard obtained in 2000 and the 22000 standard obtained in 2007 which deals with the

---

241. A definition of sustainable practices is given by Mrs Bruntland in "*Our Common Future*", a book commissioned by the United Nations for the development of the environment: "Sustainable development responds to current needs without placing in jeopardy the possibility for future generations to respond to their own needs."
242. See Chapter "The Conquest of a Global Market"…

The metronomic gyropalettes riddle the stacked bottles with balletic precision.

standardization of food safety in the global food supply chain across 120 countries. Every aspect of the Centre's work (vinification, relevant production procedures and sales) must comply with these standards. Always ahead of its time, the CV – CNF is the first company to obtain the ISO 22000 certification.

Quality, safety and the environment are all issues that are central to the Centre's plans. The CV – CNF's commitment to ethical causes is clearly evident in the multifarious measures it implements with regard to sustainable development.

In agricultural terms, the Centre advocates a "sensitive approach to winegrowing" practised by members, particularly with regard to minimising the use of fertilisers and products protecting the vines. In the first instance, ecological raw materials (labels, corks, muselet and packaging) are encouraged within the coherent framework of a "ecologically friendly policy", backed up by organic and "natural ressources". These measures are also implemented by suppliers.

The CV – CNF's respect for the environment is also reflected in its ambitious policy to reduce pollutants by optimising its transport modes. The issue of cutting greenhouse gas emissions is seriously looked into. The Centre's water treatment plant[243] reduces the amount of waste generated[244], which means that waste efficiency and reduction targets are achieved. Lastly, measures to lower the consumption of energy and water and reduce the amount of paper used are implemented. Continued research into energy efficiency has a positive effect on consumption levels which translates into a concomitant production growth edging towards the 10% mark in 2007 and 2008. Thierry Gomérieux underlines in 2009 that "The Centre Vinicole – Champagne Nicolas Feuillatte is the first company operating in the agro-alimentary industry in France to be fully committed to green

243. See Chapter "The Conquest of a Global Market".
244. The Centre opts for large containers, discarding drums made of plastic in preference to reusable containers. Sugar is now delivered in tanks as opposed to bags. Pallets can be substituted, and are therefore recyclable.

energy[245]." Other subsidiary and back up measures are endorsed, much to the CV – CNF's credit, including the recycling of cork residues which are sent to a reception centre specialised in the care of Epileptics which houses a workshop specialising in the recycling of corks with acoustic and thermal insulation[246].

Other pivotal measures taken in addition to its strategy concerning the environment concern the economic and social policies aimed at building a better future for current and future generations. The Centre has to date established mutually profitable relations with some 5,000 winegrowing members and partners of the CV – CNF. Moreover it is a highly conscientious collaborator, providing advice on technical and commercial matters and a range of services. By giving personalised advice the Centre is a great champion and defender of its region's patrimony. And by developing contacts with regional suppliers and re-distributing the wealth of quality products produced, the CV – CNF formally perpetuates the local economy.

The attainment of social equilibrium is one of the three pivotal aims of the Centre's sustainable development programme[247]. It achieves its aims by encouraging its members to preserve agricultural traditions handed down from one generation to the next. The Centre together with its winegrowers aims to ensure that agricultural crafts are preserved and shared by organising formalised training for young winegrowers and, on a more generalised level, open days covering a variety of topics (The Winegrower's Work & Quality Assurance, open days, etc.). Internally, the Centre is committed to open dialogue with its salaried staff and improving the conditions of employment by implementing the measures advised

245. Definition of green energy: it is electricity generated by clean methods as well as renewable sources of energy such as water, wind, solar rays, the heat generated by the sun, waves generated by the sea, and so on. *Le Magazine*, internal communication no. 9, March 2009.
246. The German association Diakonie Kork.
247. The economical, social and environmental axes are "the three pillars of sustainable development", as defined by the previously quoted Mrs Bruntland in 1987.

These empty bottles will soon be filled with still wine which after secondary fermentation will become champagne.

by its Health and Safety committee[248]. It encourages professional development within the organisation by setting up training programmes tailored to the individual employees' needs and offering employment opportunities to the disadvantaged. An extensive paper has been written outlining its pledge towards equal opportunities. As the statute is by definition is coherent with sustainable development, perseverance in pursuing these measures is of fundamental importance. Moreover, the position of Director of Sustainable Development has been created and it is the incumbent's duty to set up a working group to study the viability of the Centre's proposed technical and economic projects[249].

The winning of the 1st Trophée Horizon Centre Vinicole – Champagne Nicolas Feuillatte in 2009 is an eloquent tribute to the organisation's work. The prize is awarded by the French bank Crédit Agricole to suppliers demonstrating the highest levels of commitment in sustainable development[250]. Winning the award has meant not only official recognition of the Centre's genuine commitment but also of the efficiency of its policies.

These empty bottles will be filled with still wine which after secondary fermentation become Champagne.

248. The Health and Safety committee is committed to pursuing a policy for the prevention of accidents in the workplace for its employees and improving the Centre's equipment. In 2003 the board reports that the "level of serious accidents" is five times lower than the average in the profession.
249. This task delegated to the person responsible for Quality Assurance. Christophe Landat, who joined the Centre in 2006, was primarily responsible for Quality Assurance and sustainable development from 2007 onwards.
250. The CV – CNF competed with 9,000 other companies divided into three categories for the trophy: PME (petite et moyenne entreprise, small and medium sized businesses), large-scale businesses and Public Service Bodies (Établissements ou Service d'aide par le travail (ESAT).

Part three - Greater goals | PAGE 143

1 - 2 - 3. Blending still wines is a fine art. It is the grapes, crus and vintages all in different quantities that contribute towards the "goût maison" which the connoisseur recognises in each and every bottle, year after year. The vintage champagnes are an exception to the rule as they, by definition, are made with wines from a single harvest.

The role played by the cellar master in the champagne industry is of pivotal importance. Knowing everything and doing everything, his omnipresence is legendary. He monitors the way the vines grow, the quality of the grapes during the harvest and the first fermentation which he oversees with the same level of attention as one would with heating milk on the stove ...

The linchpin: the cellar master

Yet it is in his tasting of the vins clairs[251] that the cellar master comes into his own. The choices he makes are of fundamental importance. Here he embarks upon a journey of exploration; daily and over a period of several weeks he tastes each vinified wine separately according to its grape variety, naturally, but also according to the terroir it comes from and often plot by plot. Whether or not a wine makes it into the desired blend depends on its qualities at the time of the tasting. In order for the blends to work well, if the wine lacks structure, is overly acidic, lacks roundness or balance, the vins de réserve made from wine harvested earlier are used, to compensate for any weaknesses in current blends.

251. "Vin clair" is a Champagne wine that has undergone alcoholic fermentation and is then ready to be blended with other vins clairs before bottling when secondary fermentation will occur to form a frothy mousse.

After much deliberation and tasting after tasting, only the wines that once blended meet the specificities of the brand are retained. The savoir-faire needed to strike the right balance is shared by each member of the team. Under the cellar master's authority and working alongside him, the men and women of his team are there to guarantee the perpetuity of brand's distinctive flavour, the signature flavour that the consumer can enjoy year after year. The man behind the blend responsible for nearly 80% of the champagne house's production, the cellar master also assesses whether or not the fruits of the year's harvest has all the requisites of a vintage champagne. It's a difficult choice to make, and one that is dependent on several parameters, the most basic being how the wine will fare when aged. The responsibility borne by the cellar master is significant and his craft complex.

The cellar master must have considerable savoir-faire, construct, perfect and adjust his blends, but he must also be imaginative and, in boldly embracing the future, be innovative. On a human level, he manages his team, and conducts his crucially important relations with the winegrowers and everyone involved in the sector with utmost tact. Today, more so than ever before, he is called to fulfil the role of ambassador of his cuvées in his dealings with distributors and international importers. Time, that comes with experience, is evidently a factor of his success. Every year the cellar master's portfolio of knowledge is enriched and the way the wine develops corroborate the choices he makes or encourages him to work differently. Over the years he can build a homogenous range to which he can harmonise to the range of existing cuvées.

Originally, the role performed by the cellar master generally speaking working in a cooperative was different to the one fulfilled today; yet that was up until the point they decided to make their own brand. The Centre Vinicole – Champagne Nicolas Feuillatte is one of the cooperatives that makes its own brand and is one of the industry's pioneers.

As a matter of interest, it's important to remember that when the Centre Vinicole de la Champagne was set up in 1972, its primary aim was to provide storage space for its products. Jean-Pierre Daraut whose role was to manage the facility, as mentioned earlier, recalls from 1974 onwards "the need for the Centre to develop its production on an unprecedented scale, set up adequate storage facilities. This is why we planned to enlarge the Centre[252]". He believed that there was a risk that problems linked to an increase in stock would in years to come ensue, given the continued growth in vineyards and forecast rise in champagne sales. He was, in the immediate future, proved right.

There is a range of champagnes waiting to be created when Jean-Pierre Vincent takes over the reins. Little by little and year after year the cellar master of the Centre Vinicole conceives a growing number of Nicolas Feuillatte Cuvées, each of which fully satisfies the palettes of the most discerning champagne lovers.

[252]. The extraordinary general meeting report of Monday 18th February 1974.

Increasing stock levels have meant that the cellars have had to be enlarged. Today, they there is storage space for up to 100,000,000 bottles.

Again, in anticipating the CVC's ever expanding sphere of activities, there would always be demand for the development of its tank hall and cellars[253].

That is why in the early days the seven founding partners decided to appoint a manager with overall responsibility for running the tank hall. They gave the job to the technician Jacky Gaunel who came with nearly three years' experience of working at the cooperative in the village of Vincelles[254], near Dormans. "They knew about our work at the CICV laboratory, which is where I'd worked for ten years before joining Vincelles. My support for the project was boundless", says Jacky Gaunel. His role, defined by the very nature of the CVC's activities, is in essence to guarantee satisfactory storage for the stock after having overseen the harvest. Once the vinified wine is dispatched to the members, Jacky Gaunel oversees the blending of the three traditional crus in the classification of Champagne. His talents as a dégustateur are widely acknowledged and he works closely alongside Jean-Pierre Daraut. Nevertheless, stock levels are on the increase[255], and the Centre needs to increase its workforce to respond to higher production levels and build up its areas of expertise. Top of the agenda is to ensure that the high quality of the champagne it makes is maintained, and the staff stationed in the laboratory are very much in the front line.

September 1976 sees the formal appointment after having gained work experience at the CVC of a young oenologist by the name of Jean-Pierre Vincent, who joins the team headed by Jean-Pierre Daraut. Lured by the prospect of a career in the Forestry Commission, this young man hailing from Paris "who would have loved to visit the forest of Fontainebleau on horseback" dreamt of nature night and day and discovered a true passion for oenology. 1978 is the year which sees his appointment in the tank hall where he exercises his natural talents, much to the director's approval. Jacky Gaunel on the other hand does not see things the same way, "Jean-Pierre Daraut asked me to work

253. See Chapter "An avant-garde facility".
254. The Vincelles cooperative was to join the Centre Vinicole de la Champagne in 1988.
255. Stock levels increased from 30,000 to 75,000 hectolitres in four years, between 1972 and 1976 (general meeting report of 5th May 1977).

Nicolas Feuillatte has adored each and every one of the champagnes bearing his name conceived by Jean-Pierre Vincent.

alongside him, but I wasn't too keen on the idea. Why did I need a collaborator? I'd got used to working on my own," he says. And there the matter rests, and Jean-Pierre Vincent is now placed in charge of the laboratory, much to the disappointment of Yvonne Virey, who was appointed to the position when the Centre Vinicole first opened. The partnership survived just a few months up until October 1979. "I'd fractured my foot and was housebound", recounts Jacky Gaunel. Clearly unable to oversee harvest operations, the director called Jean-Pierre Vincent to the rescue, the man "Champing at the bit and itching to prove himself". With his trial run successfully accomplished, the young oenologist takes over the management of the harvest from start to finish.

When Jacky Gaunel returned to Chouilly, he was asked again if he'd be happy to work alongside an associate, particularly as things had gone so well in his absence. He refused once more. His stubbornness did not go down well with the director who once again promoted Jean-Pierre Vincent, giving him over all responsibility for the cellars and assigning Jacky Gaunel as his associate. Still bitter about the situation, but looking at things in perspective, he says, "I wasn't happy about the idea as I'd been sidelined. Nevertheless I held onto my title and carried on with my work". He knew how to do his job well in the tank hall. He was involved in the blending processes and his observations were taken into consideration during the tastings. "His ability as a taster had never been called into question", confirms the senior management. One assumes that interaction was strained and distant, with exchanges reduced to a minimum but "it wasn't a problem, everyone went about their business in their little corner, Vincent certainly wasn't throwing his weight around", a smiling Jacky Gaunel recalls. Once the wine had been bottled my work was done". This awkward state of affairs lasted for seventeen years until his departure in 1996. At just fifty five years of age Jean-Marc Pottiez, the Centre's new Chief Executive Officer informed him that he "could leave" as the legal requirements of his contract of employment had been fulfilled. This was another blow, but after giving it some thought Jacky Gaunel seized the opportunity and decided to devote himself into running full time the small 1.5 hectare vineyard owned by his family in Cramant. But all good things come to an end; he admits he's "retains happy memories of my time at the Centre", and no longer does he take his grapes to the CVC, this time he sells them to another house.

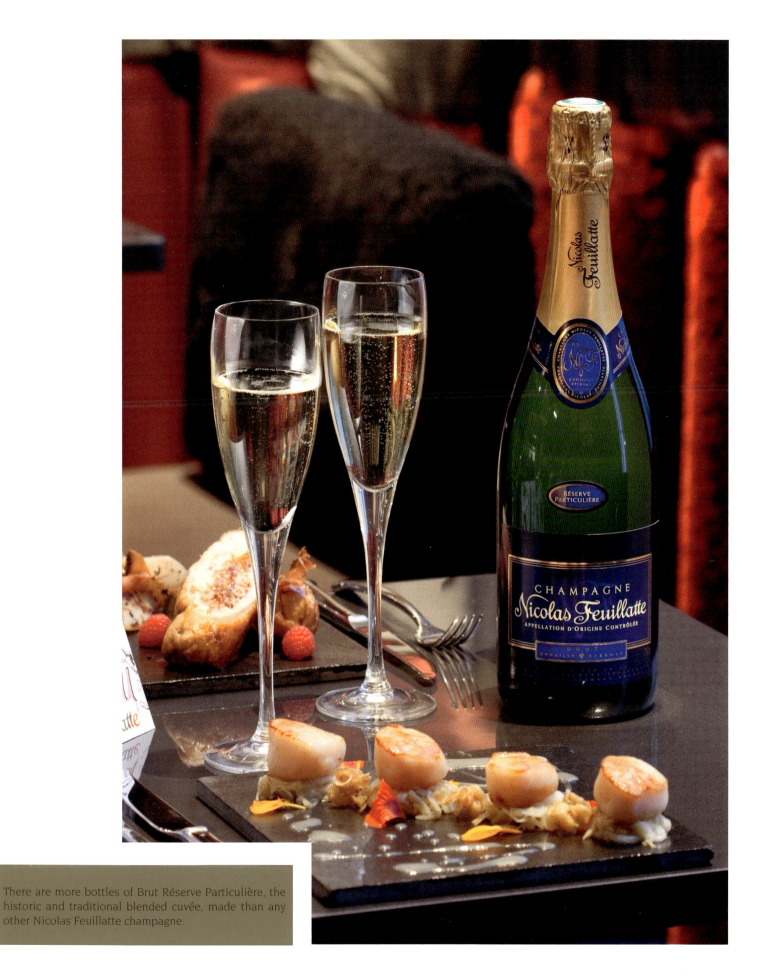

There are more bottles of Brut Réserve Particulière, the historic and traditional blended cuvée, made than any other Nicolas Feuillatte champagne.

A tasting at the Centre Vinicole – Champagne Nicolas Feuillatte.

The new responsibilities are for Jean-Pierre Vincent a godsend. He's part of an up and coming generation of oenologists who want to see their craft expand. Oenologists today want to oversee the grapes' full journey, from their arrival to the winery to putting the finished product on the market and, if appropriate, being involved in promotional activities. In short, they want overall responsibility for what goes on in the tank hall, and not just have a hand in the vinification processes. The cellar master's position can, in their opinion, be divided into three areas of responsibility. Firstly, he deals directly with the winegrowers and those responsible for winegrowing in order to choose the best grapes. Then he oversees each vinification process, ensuring they are carried out in the best possible way, and prepares the blends taking the characteristics of the year's harvest and overall requirements into account. In that respect the cellar master can intervene at any point in order to certify that each vins clair will result in the finest blends that conform to the champagne house's standards. Lastly, most importantly, he should have overall responsibility for the tastings and client contact. He should also explain the philosophy of champagne to the consumer and demonstrate its quality. His responsibilities and omnipresence make the cellar master the key person behind the brand.

There was a whole range of champagnes to make when Jean-Pierre Vincent arrived at the Centre. Step by step and little by little the cellar master of the Centre Vinicole began thinking about a growing number of Nicolas Feuillatte cuvées which would fully respond to the exacting palettes of champagne lovers all over the world. Upon his appointment, even though he did not go about broadcasting it to all and sundry, Jean-Pierre Vincent harboured ambitions to make wine he would love himself. Yet the set up he has inherited does not for the time being allow him to do so, however the future is bright. Importantly, Jean-Pierre Daraut acknowledged the qualities of this patient and reserved young man of 28, and appreciated his character as a whole. "Jean-Pierre will not disappoint", Michel Feuillat[256], his professor of oenology told him. After finishing his work experience, the move to the laboratory boosted his confidence. "I was always so impressed by the extraordinary prowess of the old masters early on in my career. They had the ability to discern which wine they were tasting and its terroir during blind tastings". The terroir Aubois de Montgueux, which he is particularly attached to, was the first to be permanently etched in his mind[257]. Yet, unlike his predecessor, Jean-Pierre Vincent loved working as part of a team, which at the time consisted of a dozen people. "Winemaking is a convivial process", he happily recalls. His dealings with the winegrowers – he loved making on-site visits to their vineyards – were cordial and over the years his visits became more frequent. But for the time being, his thirst for knowledge is unquenchable. And he knows only too well that in champagne making the way to increase one's knowledge is by creating blends.

Yet humility cannot stultify one's imagination. It just so happens that stock levels are on the increase and clearly the commercial development measures taken are working their magic, which in promotional terms can only be of benefit[258]. The top priority is to consistently improve the quality of the wine. The 1979 and 1980 cuvées given him a much appreciated opportunity. What the harvests yield over the following decade – including the harvest of 1984 – provides the cellar master with an all-consuming challenge to produce unforgettable vintages and blends resulting in superb wines.

In 1985 "Recognition of the quality improvement measures taken by the Centre has been given by commercial partners across the board[259]", much to the directors' delight. But for the time being the cuvées which are made are given to the members and sold to the off-trade; furthermore there are three specific cuvées are earmarked for exportation. But it is with the acquisition of the Nicolas Feuillatte brand the following year that a wealth of new horizons open up for Jean-Pierre Vincent. From 1986 onwards, the Centre must make in the region of 500,000 bottles of Nicolas Feuillatte Brut Réserve Particulière of which 40% are

The Cuvée 225, launched in 2005, is just one of the vintage finest quality champagnes which pairs beautifully with fine cuisine.

256. A similarity with the Nicolas Feuillatte name that Jean-Pierre Vincent has always found amusing.
257. Over time, he was soon to be able to distinguish other crus.
258. See Chapter "The Building Work"
259. Report of the general meeting of 24th May 1985.

The brut Rosé Nicolas Feuillatte makes for a particularly refined aperitif.

to be exported to foreign markets, in a bid to increase sales and sensibly control stock outflows. The brand's ambassador, Monsieur Nicolas Feuillatte throws himself wholeheartedly into the project. Moreover, supplying champagne to Mercier opens up other avenues pursued by the cellar master. "Not in terms of the quality of the wines blended by Mercier, but on measures we could take to improve the precision in our work and vinification processes", Jean-Pierre Vincent points out.

"The acquisition of the Nicolas Feuillatte brand in 1987 gave me tremendous scope for coming up with new ideas. I no longer needed to adhere to the style of old. I was at total liberty to blend the wines as I saw fit". It was in the very same year that two different but complementary worlds met. "The time was ripe for developing a simply styled champagne, accessible to all, and made with state-of-the-art vinification technology in a bid to perfect the quality of our cuvées".

Quite apart from the Brut Réserve Particulière, the Nicolas Feuillatte brand developed a prestige cuvée with the 1982 and 1983 vintages called "Palmes d'Or" in tribute to a diva close to Monsieur Nicolas Feuillatte's heart. The fact that this champagne has links with a diva is of secondary importance when considering the quality of the champagne itself. An outstanding cuvée, it has all the makings of a great champagne. It owes its exceptional character to a select blend of the finest Grands Crus and equal quantities of chardonnay and pinot noir grapes. The vintage characterising Palmes d'Or has been retained because, just like the best years, it is by definition an exceptional wine. Jean-Pierre Vincent would have preferred Palmes d'Or not to be a vintage wine "Principally because we could make a new wine every year and give it intrinsic consistency, much like Laurent-Perrier's Cuvée Grand Siècle". His idea was shelved, and this prestige cuvée is only made in only the finest vintages. Fortunately for lovers of our "divine nectar[260]", a succession of potentially vintage years starting in 1985 has resulted in the creation of several Palmes d'Or cuvées.

Quite rightly, the 1985 vintage was outstanding in Champagne. As is customary, it was the cellar master who had to decide whether or not to produce a vintage champagne in early 1986. By fortuitous coincidence, the Nicolas Feuillatte brand was acquired by the CVC and Jean-Pierre Vincent has free rein to produce a cuvée Palmes d'Or based on a new formula. The first two vintages of 1982 and 1983 were a sort of trial run. From that point on the blending of crus was cast in stone. There were five pinot noir Grands Crus selected from vineyards at Bouzy, Verzenay, Ambonnay, Aÿ and Verzy. The chardonnay is made with grapes grown in vineyards at Montgueux and the Grand Crus from Chouilly, Cramant and Mesnil-sur-Oger. The pinot noirs are well developed and structured, the chardonnays elegant with a subtle nose. Over the years the wines are perfected, evolving into veritable masterpieces. Palmes d'Or is aged in the cellars for about ten years, by which time the 1985 cuvée matures into a champagne of depth with an exceptionally well balanced bouquet, ready for release on the market, as long as the bottle is changed. The first two vintages are bottled in smooth glass and traditional flagon shaped bottles. A new bottle donning a label of understated

An impressive Nicolas Feuillatte trio: the brut Réserve Particulière, brut Millésimé and the cuvée Blanc de Blancs millésimée.

elegance replaces the traditional bottle regarded by all as too conservative[261], an adjective widely used in marketing from 1998 onwards.

"Initially, we thought we might bottle our Palmes d'Or in a crystal bottle, but the lead oxide content in lead crystal put us off the idea", says Jean-Pierre Vincent. The dark green, almost black glass of the bottle was inspired by the traditional flagon-shaped champagne

260. The adjective divine (which in the feminine is the adjective used to describe a diva) has been widely used by marketing to describe Palmes d'Or since the early 2000's.
261. The bottle was not fully discarded. A few years later it was re-instated for the Cuvée 225.

One of the latest additions to the vast range of Nicolas Feuillatte champagnes is the non dosage Brut Extrem', conceived in 2007. It is popular with a small sector of connoisseurs, particularly those from abroad, who really like the fact that no sugar is added. This characteristic is clearly spelled out on the label.

Éric Coisel, head chef at Paris' Prunier, created a unique recipe for a green lemon sorbet made with Palmes d'Or and caviar Prunier Malossol in celebration of the Palmes d'Or 1998 vintage. The combination of lemon with delicately salty caviar and unctuous Palmes d'Or is elegantly bold and innovative.

bottle. Moreover, the surface of the bottle's glass is the only one on the market which is finely pitted with tiny cavities. It has been given various nicknames[262], a clear indication of the level of interest it as generated.

It's a huge success story, the press and professionals in the field rolling out the red carpet for what they hailed as a grand cuvée.

Hubert Bruneau, the cellar master at Fauchon in Monaco "loves the cuvées that stand out from the crowd because of their original bottles", his colleague at the Cave de Beaulieu, Cedric La Horgue, believes that "Palmes d'Or Brut Vintage 1998 displays a combination of finesse and complexity and is worthy of its top-end champagne market position".

As far as cellar master Jean-Pierre Vincent is concerned he has "Conquered the Holy Grail" with Palmes d'Or millésime 1985. But the matter does not rest there. A range of cuvées hallmarked with a unique identity are in the offing.

This range includes some great classics, such as the Brut Millésimé, the Blanc de Blancs Millésimé, the Brut Rosé and the much prized Demi-Sec. Jean-Pierre Vincent has drawn inspiration from a legacy of unforgettable cuvées, which includes the three exceptional Salon 1964 magnum, Lanson 1966 magnum and Charles Heidsieck Blanc de Blancs 1982. The Blanc de Blancs was created by Daniel Thibault who Jean-Pierre Vincent admired because of his "independence and ability to turn his hand to anything[263]". Jean-Pierre Vincent followed his good example, as he much admired his unique way of working, a sine qua non component of unbridled and unhampered creativity. He saw it as an opportunity to "Break with tradition and do something new".

His personal style, the wine he wanted to make was the champagne he loves which is balanced, with a fine bead, rounded and fresh in the mouth, with an elaborate aromatic nose redolent of its terroir, complex yet displaying lightness. In short, "having finished it, you'd like to open another[264]".

The cuvée Palmes d'Or is enriched with a remarkable vintage rosé de saignée, the partner par excellence of haute cuisine.

These characteristics may appear incompatible when considering the names of the cuvées, yet they are entirely synonymous with what the wine stands for. The mission to create this special cuvée intensifies upon the arrival of president Robert on the scene,

262. The grenade is the one most popularly associated with the bottle. Is is occasionally referred to as a golf ball.
263. The cellar master at Charles and Piper Heidsieck, Daniel Thibault, passed away in 2002.
264. Yet enjoy it in moderation.

who targets foreign markets. New outlets are quick to present themselves within the context of the marketing strategy implemented by Jean-Marc Pottiez, the new director general[265].

A journalist visiting Chouilly one day is astonished by the proliferation of barrels piled up in pyramids behind enormous stainless steel tanks. A smiling Jean-Pierre Vincent deftly manoeuvres himself around them, informing the journalist that he regularly carries out "experiments and tests whilst the wines are being produced, in order to make regular assessments". Historically wood is not used in the Centre Vinicole's facility which has traditionally withstood making wines with a tannic structure. How can one explain the existence of these 225 litre capacity barrels, bought second-hand and originally used to make châblis? The journalist won't be around to see that happening and must wait for the unveiling of the mystery of the "playroom of the cellar master[266]".

Spring 2005 saw the creation of Cuvée 225, 1997 vintage. Once again, Jean-Pierre Vincent makes a wine he loves, and who is to tell him that his wine is any different from the other great wines aged in wood? "I've always wanted to do my own thing", he says. "I've always tried to create a flavour breaking away from the "Feuillatte mould", yet it had to be unique and unlike anything else on the market. I wanted it to stand out, and produce a champagne that was beefy but at the same time elegant." This explains the ageing in barrels. "Excessive youth, and therefore too much contact with wood would have unbalanced the wine" The Cuvée 225 whose name comes from the capacity of its barrels "benefits structurally from well judged barrel contact". Moreover, speaking of quality, fermentation in barrels means we can judiciously select each cru, and this improves each vine variety no end[267]. Aged for six years, our first Cuvée 225 displays great body and structure. Lastly, "in order to perfect the cuvée's balance", the cellar master decided to blend 60% of wine fermented in wood and 40% in the stainless steel tanks.

The hedonists champagne, the Cuvée 225 Rosé 2004 vintage is the logical partner to its sister in white.

Once again, the limited release of this cuvée[268] on to the market, a move much applauded by great chefs and champagne lovers and gastronomes, owes its quality to champagne crus classé. The 17 Grands Crus in Champagne account for just 8.5% of the appellation, and as a consequence are much coveted. Since the beginning of 2000 the winegrowing members of the Centre Vinicole have been producing 13 of the 17 Grands Crus, in addition to the 33 Premiers Crus out of the 42 in the Champagne appellation.

265. See Chapter "The Conquest of a Global Market"
266. The phrase coined by the Centre Vinicole – Champagne Nicolas Feuillatte tour guide, quoted in the Prologue.
267. The blend is made with equal quantities of chardonnay (crus from Chouilly, Avize, Cuis and Cramant) and pinot noir (crus from Verzenay, Bouzy, Louvois and Aÿ).
268. Some twenty thousand bottles of Cuvée 225 1997 vintage were put on the market in 2005 (retailing at 39 to 40 euros).

The temptation is too great to resist, champagne is first and foremost a wine and Jean-Pierre Vincent is lured into exploring every nook and cranny in the Region. Four Grands Crus are kept back in the outstanding year of 1995 to make a range of single varietal and single crus. Chardonnay de Cramant, Chardonnay de Chouilly, Chardonnay du Mesnil-sur-Oger and Pinot noir de Verzy. Called "Collection Particulière Grands Crus", this range[269] is ripe for expansion as, the crus that go into making them are not necessarily selected from one year to the next. Likewise, only years that are good enough to make vintage wines are considered for the range.

The bar has been set high: it's a highly specialist range and the champagne houses that have explored this avenue aimed at a connoisseur market are few and far between as the notion of terroir is somewhat alien to traditional champagne consumer culture. Champagne has for three centuries been disseminating its message on global lines, and sensibly so, as it is one of the reasons it has achieved worldwide success. Only recently did the CIVC hammer out the marketing slogan "There's not just one champagne, but champagne in general[270]", and the difference between vintage and blended brut champagne is not understood even today.

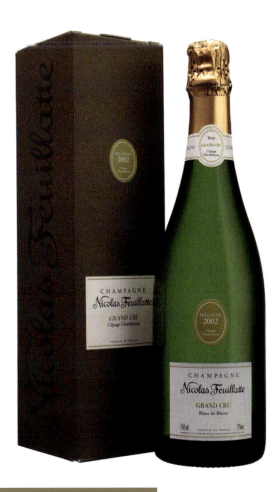

The two cuvées Grand Cru Blanc de Blancs 2002 and Blanc de Noirs 2000, made respectively with chardonnay and pinot, take over the lion's share of "Collection Particulière Grands Crus" launched in 2001. They are two of the finest crus made in Champagne.

269. The Grands Crus were launched at the 2001 VINEXPO.
270. Even though the appellation is unique.

Part three - Greater goals | PAGE 161

The concept espoused by the great chefs of today of drinking champagne throughout a meal, from starter to dessert, is new and practised only by a small minority of adventurous epicures. The Nicolas Feuillatte brand has without question been daringly developed, and all the more so as the retail price of these limited release cuvées hovers around the 30 euro mark per bottle[271]. The cuvées, much sought after by sommeliers, delicatessens and fine dining establishments, are proving their worth and carving their distinct niche in the market. Two great crus were later added to the list, the Pinot Noir d'Aÿ and the Pinot Noir d'Ambonnay[272]. 1996 was an exceptional year which enabled the cellar master and his team to produce a new selection. The renewed and amplified collection, accomplishable because of the quality of that year's wines, are hailed with much acclaim by the wineworld's élite and specialist press. Some the world's greatest chefs[273] get together to launch the Grands Crus in the Spring of 2004, to prove that they can be paired with a varied gastronomy. In 2006 the Grands Crus fall under the "Les Gourmands" classification at the Nicolas Feuillatte wine shop in Paris, with a retail unit price of 37 euros. The Chardonnay de Chouilly and Pinots d'Ambonnay millésimes 1996 are flanked by the 1997 vintages of the Grands Crus Chardonnay Cramant, Chardonnay Mesnil-sur-Oger, Pinot Noir Verzenay and Pinot Noir Aÿ. A solid marketing plan is put into play, yet the ideas behind the marketing strategy elude a vast segment of French and international consumers. The villages, apart from Bouzy with its own coq au vin recipe and the historic Aÿ, do not conjure up feelings shared in common by champagne lovers. Ambonnay does not chime with Vosne-Romanée. When it boils down to it, the winegrowers of the Champagne region simply do not have nearly as many associations to call upon as their Bourguignon neighbours.

A clear thinking Jean-Pierre Vincent veers towards presenting the spirit of his local terroir along more generalist lines by putting the grape varieties in the limelight. Consumer perception of Chardonnay and Pinot is well developed, particularly as they are much more accustomed to drinking single varietal wines from elsewhere. Consequently, foreign wine lovers look out for specific varietals.

It's business as usual in the cellars. Palmes d'Or celebrates its 20th birthday in 2005 and the first One Four see-through mini quarter bottles make their appearance on the market in the Spring. These mini bottles have been used to bottle Nicolas Feuillatte champagne since the early 1990's. Moreover Nicolas Feuillatte has been supplying Air France with champagne since 1997[274]. But the company hopes that the introduction of these new bottles retailing at 10 euros a piece will appeal to younger consumers. These handy mini bottles are ideal for brunches, pique-niques, soirées dansantes and impromptu snacks over a pair of flûtes[275]. In no time at all, Nicolas Feuillatte has exploited its image as a young, dynamic brand. Widely distributed, these mini bottles have snaffled up nearly half the quarter-bottle market[276].

Only after several years of work is a cuvée launched onto the market. And this was the case for the prestigious cuvée Palmes d'Or Rosé 1996. "It's a product I conceived myself which I couldn't be happier with that has eminently matched the specifications of my plans". Yet Jean-Pierre Vincent has set himself no mean challenge. Clearly, the cellar master's talent is revealed to the full when blending wines to produce a non vintage brut, which involves lengthy and painstaking work, yet a "rosé de saignée" demands professional prowess of a different order. When working with pinot noirs, half of which are from Riceys and the other half from Bouzy, his work must show total craftsmanship.

Despite their ruby redness, pinots are white fleshed, as is the grape juice they are made from. It is its pre-fermentary contact with the grape skins once they've

---

271. Compare this 2004 price with that of the Brut Réserve Particulière which is between 20 and 21 euros.

been harvested that gives the wine its colour. The fruit's pulp macerates in the juice which is in contact with the black-skinned grapes for the time it takes, normally a few hours, for the juice to darken. Once the cellar master decides the right colour has been attained, he then "bleeds" the cuvée, a process involving the bleeding off of the first juice from the vat to stop the pulp form imparting its colour. The coloured must can then be fermented once it has been transferred to another vat. "The difficulty in this process lies in the colour of the wine. Once macerated, the juice's deep red hues evolve bit by bit during the vinification processes into the coppery rose so typical of the Palmes d'Or Rosé 1997, passing from the brilliant and limpid ruby rose of the Palmes d'Or Rosé 1996 to the bright and deep ruby red of the Palmes d'Or Rosé 1999." This is how the wine acquires its rose-tinted hues, and it is because of the way the juice is bled that no two vintages are the same. On the other hand, the Palmes Rosé Millésimé does display specific qualities (a well defined backbone and a complex aroma including red fruits) making the wine ideal to serve with meals[277].

The Palmes d'Or Rosé 1996 vintage has been succeeded by the 1997, 1999, 2000, 2002, 2003 vintages and so on …

Now responsible for producing a range of wines demanding utmost care and attention, Jean-Pierre Vincent and his team, bolstered and galvanized by their now 30-year association with Nicolas Feuillatte champagne celebrated in 2006 are in no way fazed by attempts to produce a cuvée causing a bit of a stir in 21st Century Champagne, the brut non dosé[278]. Produced without the addition of sugar, this champagne is rapidly growing in popularity and more and more makers are producing it. Rather than being produced with dietary precautions in mind, this champagne makes for an ideal aperitif that can eloquently accompany the diner to his table. Clearly, a cuvée of this type will display a certain level of acidity and may not be to everyone's liking. Nevertheless,

The quarter white and rosé bottles One Fo(u)r were launched in 2005. Targeted at young and cosmopolitan drinkers, these mini-bottles are reminiscent of the single-serving bottles available to airline travellers.

when Nicolas Feuillatte launches its Brut Extrem' in 2007 it is specifically aiming at the foreign consumer market[279]. Suspicious of market trends and moderately enthusiastic about producing this new cuvée, Jean-Pierre Vincent is equally successful in producing a champagne he wryly defines as one that "is an ideal substitute for fresh lemon juice on oysters". Yet the Brut Extrem' is "a cuvée made for champagne lovers in search of strong stimulation leading to the discovery

272. The 6 cuvées are sold in cases of 6 at 150 euros.
273. Michel Sarran in Toulouse, Nicolas Le Bec in Lyon, Jean-Marc Banzo in Aix-en-Provence and Fumiko Kono in Paris.
274. See Chapter "The Conquest of a Global Market"
275. A quarter bottle (20 cl) is equivalent to two champagne flûtes.
276. Nielsen, annual data from 14th November 2004.
277. An alternative way of making a rosé, that is more commonly used in Champagne, is to blend in some red pinot noire wine before secondary fermentation.
278. The dosage involves adding a liqueur that contains a sugar syrup dissolved in old champagne wine. The sugar sweetens the natural acidity of wine. The amount of sugar added is strictly controlled.
279. Very dry champagne has been particularly popular in the United Kingdom since the end of the nineteenth century.

of new taste sensations". Clearly the Centre Vinicole – Champagne Nicolas Feuillatte must meet the ever growing demands of its most faithful clients, and if needs be, it should also aim to attract a new clientèle. Conscious of the fact that "Not only is this brut highly fashionable, it is in tune with the life style enjoyed by young people today in search of pure and natural products and authentic cuisine".

For Dominique Pierre, director general of the Centre Vinicole – Champagne Nicolas Feuillatte, the Brut Extrem' is "a real feather in our cap. Even though production levels might be limited[280], it is nevertheless as far as we are concerned an important product".

Fine quality grapes and a faultless vinification process go into making this cuvée. Once again the Centre Vinicole and its cellar master have risen to this latest challenge, producing a champagne that expands even further the horizons of Nicolas Feuillatte champagne. Jean-Pierre Vincent pushed the boundaries even further with the Cuvée 225 rosé. A champagne for hedonists, the wine is blended with equal quantities of pinot noir and chardonnay, topped up with a 15% to 20% content of still red wine, and vinified in barrels much in the same way as we've seen earlier. Making the Cuvée 225 Rosé 2004 was a logical step to take as she joins her counterpart in white.

Jean-Pierre Vincent scotched the rumour he was running out of ideas by launching the cuvée Grande Réserve onto the market in April 2008. Like its partners in the Nicolas Feuillatte range of cuvées, the Grande Réserve is made with the highly prestigious blend of 13 of the region's 17 Grands Crus and 33 of the 42 Premiers Crus. It is a champagne of complexity and elegance with length and freshness in the mouth.

Its key characteristic is its freshness "which is what everyone expects to find in a superb champagne". The cuvée is considered by its dégustateurs to be subtle and refined and displays a certain complexity "without being overly complicated". The appearance in 2009 of three new cuvées adds to an already richly varied range of champagnes, aptly following suit in the suite of cuvées already on the market. The vintage Grand Cru Chardonnay and Grand Cru Pinot mentioned before replace the Collection Particulière Grands Crus.

With the range of cuvées continuing to grow and the flagons multiplying, after thirty years experience Jean-Piere Vincent has been responsible for producing some 500,000,000 bottles, a record yet to be beaten by a cellar master whose dedicated his life to a single champagne house. Naturally, this achievement has been widely applauded by the wine world's press, his colleagues and contemporaries and the esteem with which he has been held by all his presidents is unanimous. Alain Robert, who has known him for six years, says of him "Jean-Pierre Vincent is a man of his time. I've been able to rely on his professional aptitude throughout, and he's never let me down". Sylvain Delaunois, who first came into contact with him when he arrived at the Centre says "The professional integrity of this man, respected by winegrowers across the board […] and creator of all our Nicolas Feuillatte cuvées, is impeccable".

The master himself in responding to this praise sends out a clear signal "The Centre's savoir-faire has gradually over time been honed by its winegrowing members who have consistently shown strength and determination in ensuring the success of our enterprise and the Nicolas Feuillatte brand. The Centre would not be where it is today without their input". Jean-Pierre Vincent's recognition of the winegrowers' work is entirely justified, and only rarely is it meted out. Jean-Pierre Vincent loves all his winegrowers, who have over the years given him so much, like one of the Centre's longest serving members, Jean Deliège from Grauves, who was part of the CVC's original team. "We've had the good fortune of working with some top oenologists. Firstly Yvonne [Virey] and then Jean-Pierre Vincent. It's been wonderful".

280. More than 8,000,000 bottles in 2006.

The *Graal* is a work based on the theme of time and was created by Guy Ferrer for Nicolas Feuillatte in 2000. Projecting out of the work is another theme, that of the never ending quest of the Holy Grail. It is a stunning tribute to the making of champagne, whose processes involve both time and courage yet also a good deal of patience and great humility.

Modestly, Jean-Pierre Vincent's response to all those congratulating him on his exceptional career, is as follows "I had no other option open to me, when you start from zero, it's all much easier".

In 2010 Jean-Pierre Vincent can, more than ever before, draw on an incredible reservoir that only a few brands have at their disposal, which account for 13 of the 17 Grands Crus in Champagne, 33 Premiers Crus out of 42 and 235 crus of the 321 made in the Champagne appellation. A major feather in his cap is Montgueux, the village in Aube he discovered whose terroir is "admired by many". This cru has traditionally never been classified, yet now it is used in a range of high quality blends made by many of the other great champagne houses. Its 25% chardonnay, 35% pinot noir and 40% pinot meunier content eminently lends itself to so many blending options.

Jean-Pierre Vincent has taken full advantage of this magnificent reservoir of crus and the Centre's state-of-the-art tank hall, bottling and tirage lines and so on that meet the requirements of its gigantic operation, which is the biggest in France, and the third largest in the world.

Yet retirement is not currently on the cards. "I've still more to achieve, but I've laid down some solid foundations", he says today, adding that "It's important we move with the times".

The works of the artists who've been in residence at the Centre since 1999 are on display, taking pride of place in the Centre Vinicole – Champagne Nicolas Feuillatte in Chouilly.

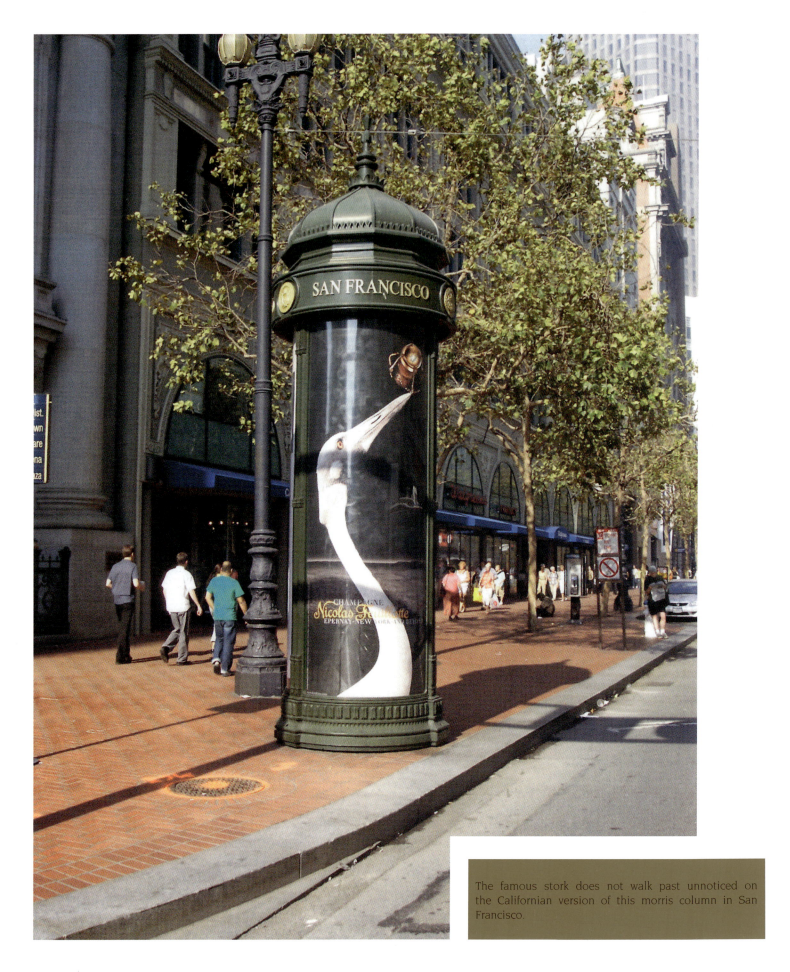

The famous stork does not walk past unnoticed on the Californian version of this morris column in San Francisco.

PAGE 168 | Nicolas Feuillatte, the champagne of the 21st Century

The image of champagne forged by the great houses of today is one closely linked to the past. Yet without abandoning its roots, the Nicolas Feuillatte brand as we know it today is firmly embedded in contemporary culture, setting the traditional wheels of communication on fire. Often represented in a refreshing way, the brand's image is at times daring, but is consistently well conceived. The Nicolas Feuillatte brand promotes a modern and dynamic image that is very much in tune with its avant-garde facility.

The Nicolas Feuillatte ad campaign is an exaltation of the Ailleurs theme which is exploited in many different ways, some quite surprising. The exotic take on the theme is based around the extraordinary world of the undersea which in 2009-2010 takes over from the wild animal motif of earlier campaigns.

Audacity and communication

"1999 was marked by a period of transition, with much thought going into conceiving a brand identity that was to be incorporated into the Centre' first publicity campaign[281]". Following the Board's instructions, Jean-Marc Pottiez and Andréa Buchin held meetings with several advertising agencies, and without a shadow of a doubt, the clear frontrunner was Callegari-Berville. Right from the very start, a mutual rapport of sincere communication was established between the agency and the Centre Vinicole's marketing team and board of directors. "Meetings were marked by reciprocal comprehension", recalls Pierre Berville[282]. "The brief[283] was clear, straightforward and clever. In fact it was so simple I was looking for hidden flaws.

281. The general meeting report of 27th April 2000.
282. Pierre Berville, senior partner in the ad agency Callegari-Berville, took charge of the Nicolas Feuillatte campaign and monitored the way it developed from beginning to end.
283. The brief was to "Tie the young Nicolas Feuillatte brand with its terroir, increase the loyalty of younger clients (35/45), flaunt its ambitions (by becoming a major player at an international level), face up to the realities of the twenty first century with conviction and not hark back to the past and recreate a false history

I kept telling myself there was a catch somewhere along the line." Experience told him that clients are always on the look out for something that would make their products stand out from the crowd. But at the end of the day, radical changes are more often than not rejected. Yet the Chouilly team know what they want and appear eager to diverge from the well trodden marketing paths of old. Jean-Marc Pottiez affirms that "Not a single brand's profile had in over

associations have not been negatively effected, in fact quite the opposite has happened.

However, large scale distribution is a growing force to be reckoned with and the great champagne labels loose no time in aiming for supermarket display stands.

No stone is left unturned when it comes to choosing publicity angles. The idea of using Abribus as a way of publicising champagne is not popular with the champagne establishment which favours

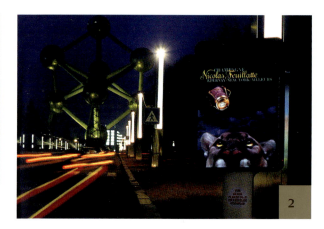

thirty years (after Laurent-Perrier) set itself apart in the Champagne industry. The big houses had always opted to perpetuate the traditional image associated with champagne drinking". Jim Galtieri, the highly energetic president of Pasternak Wine Imports in the United States notes that "The champagne world tends to operate in a somewhat conservative sphere which leans more heavily on tradition than image making and marketing". By reversing the trend, Nicolas Feuillatte caused a bit of a stir in some quarters, enthused others and managed to take the world by storm. "We need to create a new identity in a world imposing more and more restrictions. Alcohol consumption is regulated by the Loi Évin and the difficulty for us lies in promoting an image without being provocative in any way …"

The fact that the brand is distributed in all the circuits, "including those that the Champagne region does little to boast about", is yet another interesting angle for the man behind the advertising campaign to explore. This is of no concern to Nicolas Feuillatte whose brand

1 - More than 16,000 bus shelters spread across 650 towns and cities with a population in excess of 20,000 are used in the ad campaign. They're impossible to miss!.

2 - The Nicolas Feuillatte puma featured on the hoardings of Brussels, against the backdrop of the Atomium.

a more traditional approach by advertising with billboards. The marketing team at the Centre Vinicole think otherwise and do not see this option in their minds does not pose any problems "The Decaux billboards, which are well maintained and quality products provide superb visibility in prime inner city locations". And they were to be proved right, as by branching out to potentially new consumers who were confronted with the marketing message for long periods of time[284] the publicity campaign reached its target, the image is consciously and subconsciously reinforced and the Nicolas Feuillatte brand goes from strength to strength.

284. The time taken up waiting for a bus is taken into consideration, as are also the several stops en route.

3 - 4 - 5. Inaugurated in October 2007 and successor of what was originally conceived as a cellar, the Espace Nicolas Feuillatte in Paris is much more than a retail outlet. It is a place "where one can discover new champagnes and exchange ideas". Designer Christian Ghion was entrusted with transforming this contemporary space in collaboration with internationally renowned artists. This avant-garde environment beautifully sets off today's champagne.

Nevertheless the brand image needs to support a product of value and quality. "That's absolutely fundamental, as is the fact that it's important not to loose sight of the fact that luxury images tend to send out minimalist messages. We need to devise a concept that embraces the fact that a publicity works on rational, emotional and temporal levels."

Callegari-Berville immediately hit the nail on the head. "We came up with 'l'Ailleurs' as Nicolas Feuillatte champagne stands out from the crowd because of its escapist image, of travellers on a faraway voyage. The concept evokes remote shorelines attained by the sense of euphoria the drink can bring." There is a legitimate feeling of heady intoxication within this intimate sense of escapism that does not infringe the law. The marketing concept of Nicolas Feuillatte is first and foremost a hymn to "l'Ailleurs" in all its forms, even those least expected. There's an exotic element and, in that respect, featuring wild animals in the campaign can be very suggestive. And the ones chosen were beautiful, aesthetically pleasing and rare.

"The publicity campaign that featured exotic animals was a graphically stunning, highly innovative and brilliant idea." Arnaud Delbarre's[285] idea was critically acclaimed across the board and the campaign was much admired abroad. In London, Joëlle Marti[286] found it "particularly refreshing for a champagne brand". Using animals in the campaign was different and highly innovative. For the Singaporeans the campaign "symbolised a respect for nature and a blatant celebration of motherearth[287]". This analogy brings a smile to Pierre Berville's lips: "It was revolutionary."

Once the image had been cast in stone the slogans then naturally came rolling out. Initially it was "Chouilly - New York - Ailleurs", which then turned into[288] "Épernay - New York - Ailleurs". To this day the admen find the "Chouilly - New York juxtaposition a winning combination. It's just completely crazy and a fabulous oxymoron". In London[289], the slogan is interpreted "as a must". Some 400 plus taxi cabs whistling through the streets of the capital city (and Manchester) have the "foyat" animals emblazoned across their vehicles[290] for the last eight weeks of 2007. The L'ailleurs theme is exploited in alternation with the wild animal campaigns of 2000/2001, 2003/2004/2005. The travelling theme (with the hot air balloons and paddle steamers) is launched in 2006 and followed by the world of silence in 2007/2008[291]. Finally, the world of gastronomy is approached from another angle with a new take on the animal theme with an adventure into the uncharted territory of the undersea. Pumas, geckos, storks, crocodiles and flying fish and now indelibly linked with the Nicolas Feuillatte corks, clothed in their foil hood and muselet[292].

4

285. Arnaud Delbarre, quoted in the Chapter "An Eye to the Future?"
286. Joëlle Marti, Great Eastern Hotel, London.
287. Roderic Proniewski, Parker Wines, Singapore.
288. It has already been mentioned that the marketing men favoured Épernay because of its international fame. See Chapter "The Conquest of a Global Market".
289. *Give me the best or nothing!*. Joëlle Marti (see footnote 286). In London the strap line "Épernay – New York – Ailleurs" is suavely translated into "Epernay – London – Beyond".
290. In English-speaking countries, Feuillatte is pronounced "Foyat". The American website sayitfoyat.com is a humorous play on words.
291. The Nicolas Feuillatte cork nestles inside a piece of coral or a strange colony of sea anemones.
292. However, the new-look champagne bottle makes its appearance for the very first time in 2010.

The designer Christian Ghion has worked on a number of projects for Nicolas Feuillatte champagne.

The brand is marketed in airports, Abribus and phone booths. In 2010 Nicolas Feuillatte champagne takes to the Paris métro, with posters standing alongside those of tour operators tempting hopeful travellers with faraway destinations.

The image of Nicolas Feuillatte champagne is displayed across a variety of media, including national and international magazines and internet podcasts, all this quite apart from the billboard campaigns. The packaging, accessories and objects associated with champagne designed by designers of world renown[293] are part of the "complete deal" and an elegant and unique communications strategy. The champagne is dramatically presented in the Espace Nicolas Feuillatte in Paris. This space, which had previously been La Cave Nicolas Feuillatte is more than just a retail outlet. It's a space "where one can discover new champagnes and exchange ideas".

Originally conceived as a traditional "boutique-cave-vitrine" for the brand, the board is very much in favour of this Parisian space's new purpose, situated in a prime location just moments away from the Champs-Élysées in the internationally known Rue du Faubourg-Saint-Honoré. The board entrust the design concept of the site to Christian Ghion[294], who gives the space greater prominence. Opened in October 2007, the Espace Nicolas Feuillatte is an iconic building of its time, indeed several contemporary artists have had a hand in its conception. It is in effect an elegant and avant garde reflection of a modern champagne. Black predominates as it is the colour most emblematic of contemporary luxury in this space that exudes naturalness and quality, and flaunts its glass and polished rosewood and pure lines evoking a refined universe. The enchanted visitor navigates his way

---

293. Including Yan Pennors, Hervé Van der Stracten, Christian Ghion …
294. Christian Ghion, architect and designer is most known for having designed Pierre Gagnaire's restaurants in Paris and Tokyo, the fashion designer shops of Chantal Thomass and Castelbajac, the Marionnaud stores and the Comité Colbert exhibition space in Shanghai 2006. The artist, who has been working with Nicolas Feuillatte since 2000, also designed the *Cocoon* champagne bucket and other equipment used to keep champagne chilled.

In responding to the 1999 theme based on "Le Terroir", Marie Thurman is the first in a long line of artists and photographers of international renown to offer a visual translation of the Feuillatte universe.

L'Espace by Tony Soulié (2001).

PAGE 176 | Nicolas Feuillatte, the champagne of the 21st Century

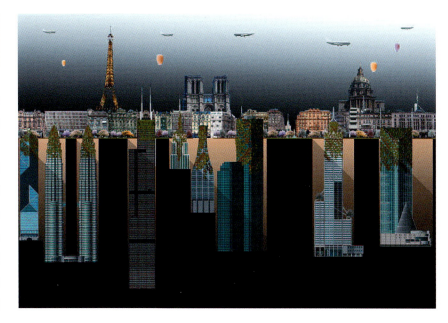

Le Temps et l'Espace by Édouard François (2007).

through the several bottles displayed like works of art on pillars and glass cabinets. This helps to create the overall tone of the space.

The association between the Nicolas Feuillatte brand and contemporary art continues, with its patronage of artists' avant garde work. The idea of associating Nicolas Feuillatte champagne with contemporary art came about in the late 1990's, when the company embarked upon a new and innovative publicity campaign[295]. "The ramifications took on an added dimension in 2002 with the institution of the "Prix Nicolas Feuillatte pour l'Art contemporain", awarded annually to the artist who works on the brand's concept[296]." The "Prix Jeune Espoir Nicolas Feuillatte" was instituted in very much in the same spirit, to the "artists of the future", and is awarded each year to a student enrolled at the École nationale des beaux-arts de Paris.

In 2002 the Chouilly brand was once again the champagne served at FIAC[297], and since clinching that deal it has been the exclusive champagne served at some of the world's most prestigious institutions such as the Centre Pompidou in Paris, London's Tate Modern, New York's MoMa, the Mori Art Museum in Tokyo, Milan's Accademia delle Belle Arti di Brera and Munich's Pinakothek der Moderne. The brand has also been the official partner of ArtParis since 2006, the international art fair held in Paris's Grand Palais, which is further evidence of its commitment to contemporary art.

Its commitment is blatantly obvious in the Chouilly cellars of the Centre Vinicole - Champagne Nicolas Feuillatte where the works of the artist in residence have been on display since 1999. Marie Thurman was the first in a long line of internationally acclaimed artists and photographers to have since 1999 endeavoured to recreate the Feuillatte universe through her work when she rose to the challenge to produce a work of art on the theme of *Le Terroir*.[298] Her successors were Guy Ferrer (*le temps*), Tony Soulié (*l'espace*), Philippe Favier (*terres d'ailleurs*), Bruno Bressolin (*sans frontières*), Marc Comes (*L'Effervescence*), Donna Trope (*skin contact*), Tanguy Loyzance (*dream travel*), Édouard François (*Paris 2050: un voyage dans le temps*), Marina Fedorova (*Moment unique*), Aspassio Haronitaki (*Effervescence*), Nils-Udo (*Nature: éruption d'été*) … playful and poetic themes continue to ebb and flow, and though the inspiration behind the theme may be repeated (le temps, l'effervescence, l'ailleurs), it does not mean that the works that emerge will be any the less unique.

These highly apt artistic manifestations, included in which are the creations of François Gingembre who is fascinated by gastronomic combinations using spices, the l'Ailleurs theme, and the designers' work discussed earlier, continue today and all contribute towards perpetuating an innovative image of champagne.

One must constantly strive for perfection in order to conquer; high level team sport players and the adeptness of sailors are prime examples. It is totally

---

295. See Chapter "The Conquest of a Global Market"
296. *Le Magazine*, special 30th anniversary edition, December 2006.
297. Pommery had been the champagne served up until 2001 at this international contemporary art fair.
298. See Chapter "The Conquest of a Global Market".

understandable that Nicolas Feuillatte, in laying claim to its firm footing on the market, is enjoyed by world champions competing at international level. Staunch partnerships have naturally formed, such as that with Michel Desjoyeaux, a great lover of champagne who confides that "Only Nicolas Feuillatte[299] will do at the big events". The response to "what are the connections in common between sailing and the Nicolas Feuillatte brand?", is "The quality of the spray, of course!" so replies with good humour the winner of several competitions, who then showing no hesitation adds "On a more serious note, efficacy and integrity". This fitting tribute has been echoed by a good many other world champions, including Raphaël Nadal, Yannick Noah, Fabien Pelous, Jérôme Proux[300].

"The brand stands out from the crowd by emphasising not only its youth and dynamism,
but also its exuberance and nerve.", says Henri Jobbé Duval, Director of ArtParis. Also singing
the brands praises are Michael Shuster and Norman Gladstone[301], who say that "the youth and dynamism of this brand of modern champagne is highly alluring", and in their opinion "it is these two characteristics that have led to the brand's success".

Given the track record, what's also needed is a certain boldness continue to show the same innovative spirit. And since 1972 the founders of the Centre Vinicole - Champagne Nicolas Feuillatte have had plenty of that.

299. Interview with *Magazine,* December 2006.
300. Respective winners of the Swedish Open in 2005, Davis Cup 1991, captain of the French national Rugby team in 2004, and horse jumping in Bordeaux in 2001.
301. Founder directors of International Cellars in 1983 (Western Canada)...

Terres d'Ailleurs by Philippe Favier (2002).

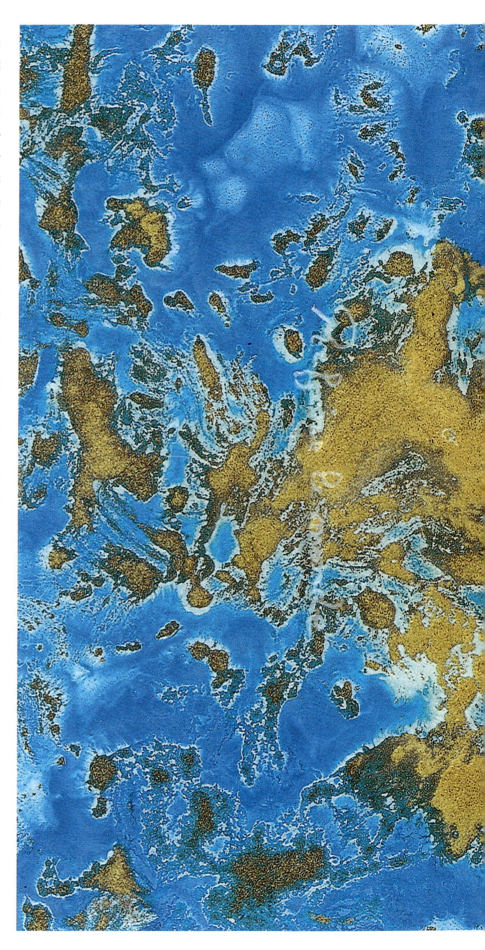

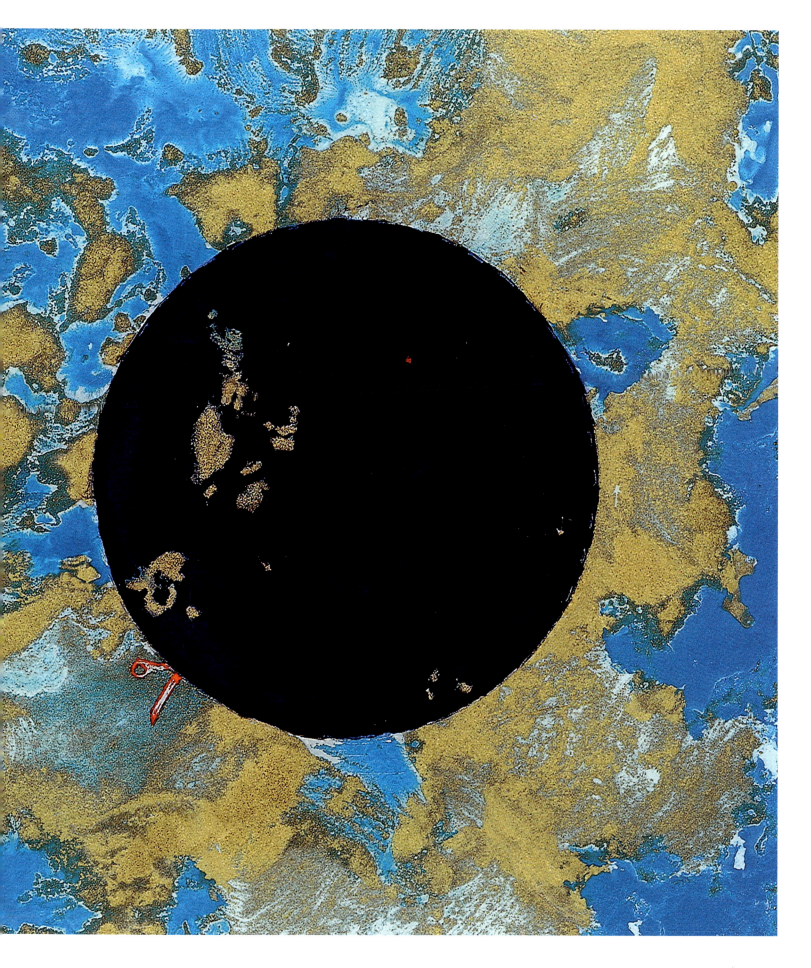

1 - *Sans frontières* by Bruno Bressolin (2003).
2 - *Effervescence* by Aspassio Haronitaki (2008).

Part three - Greater goals | PAGE 181

PAGE 182 | Nicolas Feuillatte, the champagne of the 21st Century

1 - *Skin Contact* by Donna Trope (2005).
2 - *Moment Unique* by Marina Fedorova (2009).
3 - *Éruption d'été* by Nils-Udo (2010).

REFERENCES:

BOOKS:

- *Le Livre d'or du champagne*, François Bonal, Éditions du Grand-Pont, Lausanne, 1984
- *Les Vins de Champagne*, André Garcia, PUF, 1986, 1997
- *100 ans d'unité syndicale, 1904-2004*, Yves Chauvé, 2004

PRESS:

- *La Champagne viticole*
- *Les Échos*
- *La Marne agricole*
- *Le Nouvel Observateur*
- *L'Union*
- *Le Vigneron champenois*

WEBSITE:

- *Une histoire de la Champagne*, index of champagne houses and people involved in the industry, http//max.buvry.free.fr/

ACKNOWLEDGEMENTS:

Many of Monsieur Nicolas Feuillatte's associates have been more than happy to recount the intriguing story behind the Centre Vinicole - Champagne Nicolas Feuillatte. I thank them all most warmly. The biggest thanks of all must go to Monsieur Sylvain Delaunois and Dominique Pierre, respectively President and Director General of the CV – CNF for their heartfelt wish to see this book come to fruition.

My thanks also to:
Jean-Pierre Vincent, cellar master and Jean-Pierre Daraut, Director General of the CV - CNF (1972-1993), Alain Robert, President (1993-2000), Jean Deliège and André Patis, former board members and founders of the Centre, Serge Rafflin, Jean-Marc Pottiez, Director General of the CV - CNF (1994-2001), René Baccot, Michel Foutrier and Jacky Gaunel for their first hand accounts and Pierre Delville for his insight into the Nicolas Feuillatte communication policy, Nadine Leroy, highly regarded CV – CNF collaborator, for her efficient research, Alexandrine Legras-Populus of the Fédération des coopératives vinicoles de Champagne, Xavier Muller and Jean-François Préau, respectively president and director general of Champagne Mailly Grand Cru, Nathalie Costa, editor-in-chief of *La Champagne viticole*, Lara Fournier-Pinçon, Valérie Kéréver, Émilie Jeangeorges and everyone else who has supported me in the creation of this book.

My thanks to Aleksandra Sokolov who without hesitation decided to produce this book and publish it as part of the Thalia Édition "Patrimony" series, and to Aurore Markowsky, of Magraphiste, who has performed the most worthy task of typesetting my texts.

NOTA BENE:

Some of the names published here begin with capital letters in accordance with professional and geographic practices.

Treat alcohol responsibly…

INDEX :

p.1:
The Nicolas Feuillatte Cork, 2010
© Baptiste Heller.

p.3-4:
The Nicolas Feuillatte Cork, 2010
© Baptiste Heller.

p.5:
Cuvée Millésime.
© GrantSYMON

PREFACE:

p.6:
Nicolas Feuillatte.
© Nicolas Feuillatte, Chouilly.

PART 1:

p.10-11:
Harvest time at Aÿ, press cutting from c. 1900
© Archives A. Markowski.

p.12:
Paris illustré, front cover 5 novembre 1887 drawn by the artist Maybach.
© Archives A. Markowski.

p.13:
The rolling hills of Aÿ, postcard.
© Archives A. Markowski.

p.14:
Alphonse Perrin.
© La Champagne vinicole.

p.15, left:
Émile Michel-Lecacheur.
© La Champagne vinicole.

p.15, right:
Gaston Poittevin.
© La Champagne vinicole.

p.16:
Maurice Doyard.
© La Champagne vinicole.

p.17:
Harvest time in Champagne – the grape pickers.
Postcard (private collection).
© Archives A. Markowski.

p.18:
Winegrowers and cooperative members, photo, circa 1930.
© Mailly Grand Cru.

p.19:
Robert-Jean de Vogüé.
© Collection Moët & Chandon.

p.20, top right:
Henri Macquart.
© Nicolas Feuillatte, Chouilly.

p.20, bottom left:
Jean Nollevalle.
© La Champagne vinicole.

p.21:
The grape presser…,

p.251, *Le Monde illustré,* 17 October 1908.
© Archives A. Markowski.

p.22:
Front cover, *Le Monde illustré,* 17 Octobre 1908.
© Archives A. Markowski.

p.22-23:
Harvest time in Champagne, getting the grapes ready for pressing… front cover, *Le Monde illustré,* 17 October 1908.
© Archives A. Markowski.

p.24-25:
Singing joyful songs…,

p.251, *Le Monde illustré* 17 October 1908.
© Archives A. Markowski.

p.26:
Taking the grapes to be pressed in the Autumn.
The CIVC picture library.
© John Hodder.

p.29:
The wine regions of Champagne.
© The CIVC picture library.

p.30:
Henry Macquart.
© Nicolas Feuillatte, Chouilly.

p.33:
A Harvest
© Nicolas Feuillatte, Chouilly.

p.36-37:
The Building Site, Centre Vinicole de la Champagne, Spring 1972.
© Nicolas Feuillatte, Chouilly.

p.38:
The Building Site, Centre Vinicole de la Champagne, Spring 1972.
© Nicolas Feuillatte, Chouilly.

p.39:
The Building Site, Centre Vinicole de la Champagne, Spring 1972.
© Nicolas Feuillatte, Chouilly.

p.40:
The vines of Hautvillers.
The CIVC picture library.
© Claude et Françoise Huyghens Danrygal.

p.41:
The Building Site, Centre Vinicole de la Champagne, 1972.
© Nicolas Feuillatte, Chouilly.

p.42:
The Building Site, Centre Vinicole de la Champagne, 1972.
© Nicolas Feuillatte, Chouilly.

p.47, above:
Inauguration of the Centre, 7 July 1978.
© Nicolas Feuillatte, Chouilly.

p.47, below:
Centre Vinicole de la Champagne, 1978.
© Nicolas Feuillatte, Chouilly.

p.48-49:
The Inauguration, 7 July 1978.
© Nicolas Feuillatte, Chouilly.

p.50-51:
The Extension of the Centre Nicolas Feuillatte
being built,
June-July 1981.
© Nicolas Feuillatte, Chouilly.

p.52:
The vines and parish church at Chavot in the autumn against a grey sky, 1993.
The CIVC picture library.
© Visuel Impact.

p.53:
Frosted trees and vines, 1981
The CIVC picture library.
© Frédéric Hadengue.

p.55:
Serge Rafflin.
© Nicolas Feuillatte, Chouilly.

p.56, left:
Serge Rafflin in his vineyard.
© Private Collection.

p.56, right:
Serge Rafflin with his son Denis at a tasting.
© Private Collection.

p.60-61:
The Vineyard pictured in the Autumn setting sun, 1993.
The CIVC picture library.
© Visuel Impact.

p.62-63:
Bottles in the Nicolas Feuillatte cellar.
© Michel Jolyot.

p.64:
The Nicolas Feuillatte labelling line.
© Michel Jolyot.

p.65:
Centre Vinicole de la Champagne, 1986.
© Brand Image.

p.68:
Dinner at Windsor Castle…, 1991.
© Nicolas Feuillatte, Chouilly.

p.69:
Un après-midi à Hammamet…
© Nicolas Feuillatte, Chouilly.

p.71:
Jacques Anquetil in front of the Centre Vinicole de la Champagne, May 1987.
© Nicolas Feuillatte, Chouilly.

p.72:
Espace Nicolas Feuillatte.
© François Maréchal.

p.74-75:
Bottles of Nicolas Feuillatte Champagne.
© Michel Jolyot.

p.76:
The tank hall at night.
© Brand Image.

p.77:
Champagne: bunches of white grapes boxed up after the harvest, September 1996.
The CIVC picture library.
© John Hodder.

p.78:
Nicolas Feuillatte and
Alain Robert.
© Nicolas Feuillatte, Chouilly.

p.81:
Alain Robert.
© Nicolas Feuillatte, Chouilly.

p.83:
Jean-Pierre Daraut and
Nicolas Feuillatte.
© Nicolas Feuillatte, Chouilly.

p.84:
Jean-Marc Pottiez and Alain Robert.
© Nicolas Feuillatte, Chouilly.

p.85:
Champagne Bottles in the Nicolas Feuillatte Cellar.
© Michel Jolyot.

PART II:

p.86-87:
Picnic hamper.
© Nicolas Feuillatte, Chouilly.

p.88:
The stainless steel tanks, Nicolas Feuillatte.
© Michel Jolyot.

p.89:
A London Cab, 2007.
© Nicolas Feuillatte, Chouilly.

p.90.
The Nicolas Feuillatte Champagne labelling line.
© Michel Jolyot.

p.91:
The Nicolas Feuillatte Gyropalettes.
© Michel Jolyot.

p.93:
Air Tahiti Nui Cabin Crew member.
© Nicolas Feuillatte, Chouilly.

p.96:
The Nicolas Feuillatte Signature and strapline.
© Nicolas Feuillatte, Chouilly.

p.97:
Advertising in New York.
© Nicolas Feuillatte, Chouilly.

p.99:
An exhibition of art works at the Centre Vinicole – Champagne Nicolas Feuillatte.
© Nicolas Feuillatte, Chouilly.

p.100-101:
Harvest time in Champagne, September 1996.
The CIVC picture library.
© John Hodder.

p.102-103:
The Seychelles Regata.
© p.Jaffredou & G. Kazade.

p.104:
Christian Labit, Nicolas Feuillatte and Jean-Louis Jourdan.
© Nicolas Feuillatte, Chouilly.

p.105:
Raphael Nadal winner of the Swedish Open, 2005.
© Nicolas Feuillatte, Chouilly.

p, 106:
Michel Desjoyeaux and his team members, 8 July 2004.
© Nicolas Feuillatte, Chouilly.

p.107:
Jacques Girod, Jean-Marc Pottiez and Serena Williams, 2000.
© Nicolas Feuillatte, Chouilly.

p.108:
Sylvain Delaunois.
© Nicolas Feuillatte, Chouilly.

p.109:
Sylvain Delaunois and Dominique Pierre.
© Nicolas Feuillatte, Chouilly.

p.111:
Dominique Pierre and Fabien Pelous.
© Nicolas Feuillatte, Chouilly.

p.112:
Marc Comes.
Stills from a DVD based on the effervescence theme, 2004.
© Nicolas Feuillatte, Chouilly.

p.113:
Jean-Pierre Vincent and Fumiko Kono.
© Nicolas Feuillatte, Chouilly.

p.114, top left:
Olivier Roëllinger and Dominique Pierre.
© Nicolas Feuillatte, Chouilly.

p.114, top right:
Enrico Bernardo and Olivier Poussier.
© Nicolas Feuillatte, Chouilly.

p.117:
The performers of Cirque Pinder, 2006.
© Nicolas Feuillatte, Chouilly.

p.119:
The Nicolas Feuillatte Champagne labelling line.
© Michel Jolyot.

p.120-121:
The Nicolas Feuillatte tank hall.
© Michel Jolyot

p.122:
The Nicolas Feuillatte tank hall.
© Michel Jolyot.

p.123:
A tasting chez Nicolas Feuillatte.
© Nicolas Feuillatte, Chouilly.

p.124:
The Vineyards of Champagne in Spring, Mesnil-sur-Oger.
The CIVC picture library.
© John Hodder.

p.127, top right:
Brooklyn Bridge, New York.
© Photos.com.

p.127, bottom left:
A bottle of Nicolas Feuillatte champagne in front of the Sydney Opera House.
© Nicolas Feuillatte, Chouilly.

p.127, middle top:
Rio de Janeiro.
© Photos.com.

p.127, middle bottle:
The Great Wall of China.
© Photos.com.

p.127, top right:
Moscow.
© Photos.com.

p.127, bottom right:
Mount Fuji, Japan.
© Photos.com.

p.128:
Sylvain Delaunois in his vineyards.
© Nicolas Feuillatte, Chouilly.

p.130-131:
Tanguy Loyzance, *Dream Travel*, photomontage, 2006.
© Nicolas Feuillatte, Chouilly.

PART III:

p.132-133:
Bowl.
The Christian Ghion and Nicolas Feuillatte Collection.
© Fillioux & Fillioux.

p.134:
Nicolas Feuillatte tin foil.
© Michel Jolyot.

p.135:
The Nicolas Feuillatte Bottling Line.
© Michel Jolyot.

p.136, left and right:
The Nicolas Feuillatte Laboratory.
© Nicolas Feuillatte, Chouilly.

p.137:
Bottling Line Nicolas Feuillatte.
© Michel Jolyot.

p.138, above and below:
Bottling Line Nicolas Feuillatte.
© Michel Jolyot.

p.139:
Nicolas Feuillatte barrels.
© Michel Jolyot.

p.140:
Nicolas Feuillatte gyropalettes.
© Michel Jolyot.

p.141:
Handling the Nicolas Feuillatte Champagne bottles.
© Michel Jolyot.

p.142-143:
The Nicolas Feuillatte Bottling Line.
© Photo Michel Jolyot.

p.144-145:
The Blending: The Table.
© Nicolas Feuillatte, Chouilly.

p.146:
The Blending.
© Nicolas Feuillatte, Chouilly.

p.147:
The Blending: glasses.
© Nicolas Feuillatte, Chouilly.

p.148:
Jean-Pierre Vincent.
© Xavier Lavictoire.

p.149:
The Nicolas Feuillatte Cellars.
© Michel Jolyot.

p.150:
Nicolas Feuillatte and Jean-Pierre Vincent.
© Nicolas Feuillatte, Chouilly.

p.151:
Réserve Particulière, back to magic.
© OMG2.

p.152:
A Tasting at the Centre Vinicole – Champagne Nicolas Feuillatte.
© Nicolas Feuillatte, Chouilly.

p.153:
Cuvée 225.
© De Visu.

p.154-155:
Brut Rosé, rosé bubbles in Paris rose
© Olivier Martin Gambier.

p.156, left:
Chardonnay Blanc de Blancs.
© De Visu.

p.156, top right:
Réserve particulière.
© De Visu.

p.156, bottom right:
Millésime 1999.
© De Visu.

p.157:
Brut Extrem'.
© GrantSYMON.

p.158:
Palmes d'Or, vintage 1998.
Nicolas Feuillatte at Prunier in Paris, 18 June 2008.
© Nicolas Feuillatte, Chouilly.

p.159:
Cuvée Palmes d'Or, vintage 2004 Rosé.
© Nicolas Feuillatte, Chouilly.

p.160:
Jean-Pierre Vincent, Cuvée 225 Rosé millésime 2004.
© Nicolas Feuillatte, Chouilly.

p.161:
Cuvées Grand Cru Blanc de Blancs 2002 and Blanc de Noirs 2000.
© Nicolas Feuillatte, Chouilly.

p.163:
The mini quarter bottles One Fo(u)r, 2005.
© Nicolas Feuillatte, Chouilly.

p.165:
Guy Ferrer, *Le Graal, oil on canvas.*
© Nicolas Feuillatte, Chouilly.

p.166-167:
Exhibition of art works at the Centre Vinicole – Champagne Nicolas Feuillatte.
© Michel Jolyot.

p.168:
A Morris column in San Francisco.
© Nicolas Feuillatte, Chouilly.

p.169:
Green Anemone (detail from a Nicolas Feuillatte ad).
© Focale 3 Reims.

p.170, left:
Abribus, Gecko, Paris.
© Nicolas Feuillatte, Chouilly.

p.170, right:
Abribus, Puma, Brussels.
© Nicolas Feuillatte, Chouilly.

p.171:
Espace Nicolas Feuillatte.
© Alain Longeaud.

p.172:
Espace Nicolas Feuillatte (shop window).
© François Maréchal.

p.173:
Christian Ghion.
Collection Christian Ghion and Nicolas Feuillatte.
© Fillioux & Fillioux.

p.174-175:
Marie Thurman, *Le Terroir*, 1999.
© Nicolas Feuillatte, Chouilly.

p.176:
Tony Soulié, *L'Espace*, 2011.
© Nicolas Feuillatte, Chouilly.

p.177:
Édouard François, *Le Temps et l'Espace*, 2007.
© Nicolas Feuillatte, Chouilly.

p.178-179:
Philippe Favier, *Terres d'Ailleurs,* 2002.
© Nicolas Feuillatte, Chouilly.

p.180:
Bruno Bressolin, *Sans Frontières*, 2003
© Nicolas Feuillatte, Chouilly.

p.181:
Aspassio Haronitaki, *Effervescence*, 2008.
© Nicolas Feuillatte, Chouilly.

p.182.
Donna Trope, *Skin Contact*, 2005.
© Nicolas Feuillatte, Chouilly.

p.183:
Marina Fedorova, *Moment unique*, 2009.
© Nicolas Feuillatte, Chouilly.

p.184-185:
Nils-Udo, *Éruption d'été*, 2010.
© Nicolas Feuillatte, Chouilly.

p.192:
The Nicolas Feuillatte Cork, 2010.
© Baptiste Heller.

Despite every effort having been made to trace and obtain permission for the use of copyright material, we cannot accept responsibility for any errors herein. The editor apologises for any such oversights and asks for anyone concerned to contact the publishing house in order to redress the situation.

Thalia Édition
www.thaliaedition.com

Print in Italy by L.E.G.O. S.P.A. Lavis (TN), Fèvrier 2012.

www.thaliaedition.com